ALL AHEAD FULL

How to Navigate Your Way to a Great Life

John Mann

ISBN: 1-4196-9228-3
ISBN-13: 9781419692284

Visit www.booksurge.com to order additional copies.

Dedication

First of all, I would like to thank Wendy Gill with Professional Communications in Matthews, North Carolina for believing in *All Ahead Full* and for wanting to be a part of this project. Believe me, the book reads much better due to her assistance!

I dedicate this book to the many people who have influenced my life over the years. First of all, to my mom Barbara Barnett, who made sure that I always made it to church even when we barely had enough money to pay for gas. To my dad Jim Mann, who passed away a few years ago but taught me the value of hard work. To my sisters and brother DurRinda Mix, RaDonna Scroggins, and James Mann, who have been the best siblings for whom anyone could ever ask. To my business partners Jeff Hensley, Joel Barham, Hobert Corbett, and Wendy Mason, who I have been blessed to work with for many years. To Edward Bruette, who inspired this book in the first place—his leadership completely changed my life. And last but certainly not least, my wife Maggie, who has been my shipmate for over twenty-two years. Thanks for making this journey so much fun!

DEPARTMENT OF THE NAVY

From: G.L. Wolverton (Commanding Officer, USS Stonewall Jackson SSBN Gold Crew)
To: Chief of Naval Education and Training

Subject: QM3 (SS) John Alan Mann

During the period that Quartermaster Mann has served as a member of our crew he has exhibited exacting professionalism in technical knowledge of Practical Navigation and his SUPERIOR good judgment during many hazardous maneuvering situations; whether traveling up the treacherous St. Mary's River to Kings Bay Naval Submarine Base or piloting less familiar waters, his extremely competent and highly professional manner turned hazardous routes into routine maneuvers. He has performed in an environment of great stress and has been required to make time sensitive decisions under these circumstances. In every instance he proved that he had the ability to make excellent judgments. Using his own initiative and *take charge* attitude he has made major contributions to the safe navigation of the USS Stonewall Jackson for over twenty-five thousand miles of transit.

I want it known that I believe Petty Officer Mann is a Superior Petty Officer and is capable of becoming an OUTSTANDING officer for the United States Navy. It is my recommendation that he be given an opportunity to attend a Boost Program and then be sent to Officer Candidate School.

Contents

Please note that while all of these chapters have nautical themes the content in each relate to making your personal, professional, and spiritual, life the best it can be!

Introduction

There is absolutely nothing in my background to suggest that I would become one of the youngest primary submarine navigators in U.S. history. Likewise, there is nothing at all to suggest that I would help create one of the most successful food brokerage companies in the country.

I spent many years growing up on a modest, 90-acre family farm in Quapaw, Oklahoma. We owned a small number of chickens, cows, horses, and pigs, and I spent my time milking, painting, pitching hay, running barbed wire, and shucking corn. Money was always in short supply, yet I never worried about clothing, food, or shelter. For several years our family of five (sister DurRinda had already left home) lived in a single-wide trailer on the farm. I'll admit that we had our share of excitement there, since Quapaw is in northeastern Oklahoma, otherwise known as Tornado Alley.

During the mid-1970s, most children in Quapaw weren't brought up to think about college educations. Most of my friends expected to become electricians, mechanics, store clerks, truck drivers or farmers. But none of these professions interested me. I had no idea what I wanted to be, but I knew for sure that I wanted to look for something outside of our tiny town.

My older brother had already found his way out of Quapaw through the Marine Corp. While still in high school, I chose my own way out. I joined the Navy.

Back in those days, the only thing I had going for me was a decent amount of common sense. I was as green as they come. But it wasn't my inexperience that held me back during my earliest months in the military; it was something I didn't even recognize at the time. It was an unseen enemy that hides where many of us don't care to go—inside ourselves. The enemy for me was *doubt*.

Fortunately, Chief Edward Bruette encouraged me to stare that enemy straight in the eyes. During my four years in the Navy, Bruette expertly taught me how to navigate submarines and, in the process, taught me how to navigate life. He inspired self-confidence and provided a reliable chart for success. Thanks to Bruette's lessons, my unpromising life gradually began to change course.

Decades later, I credit much of my success in business to him. My company, SellEthics Marketing Group, Inc., began as a small company with two clients and barely enough sales to cover payroll and expenses. Eight short years later, we have more than one hundred clients, more than three hundred and fifty employees and annual sales of well over $500 million!

Even more importantly, I've experienced great happiness in my personal life. I'm grateful to have enjoyed over twenty-two years of marriage with my wonderful wife, Maggie.

The odds were stacked against me in that area, too. I met my future father-in-law, a retired two-star Army general, while I was still in the Navy. He sternly advised his daughter not to marry me, in part because I murdered the King's English. (He and I both laugh about that today.) Even some of my military buddies told Maggie that I was an ignorant farm boy who was never going to amount to anything.

Here's the point: if a so-called country bumpkin like myself can achieve remarkable personal and professional success, you can, too. I consider it a privilege to pass on some of the lessons that have supported my journey.

The title of this book, *All Ahead Full*, is a nautical term used when a ship or submarine is in open waters. It signals that the time is right to open up the throttles and let her rip! *All Ahead Full* applies to our lives as well. Life is a ship; and each of us is designed to travel from one destination (or goal) to the next.

Unfortunately, too many of us are missing the boat. We keep ourselves tied to the pier rather than venture out to sea. *All Ahead Full* is about letting go of whatever holds you back. It's about allowing your life to open up to new experiences and adventures.

So, let's pull up anchor and discover how to proceed ... *all ahead full!*

Boot Camp

Boot camp: All enlisted personnel are required to attend a boot camp at the start of their military career. Boot camp typically runs from eight to twelve weeks and serves as a transition from civilian life to military life.

Boot camp has never been known for its warmth and friendliness. But, it sure taught me a lot.

It was January 1981, during my senior year in high school, that I joined the Navy. Only eight days after graduation, I was at a Greyhound bus station saying final goodbyes to my family and friends. My mother held back tears (I'm assuming sadness rather than joy) as she put her baby-faced boy on the bus. Though I put on a brave front, I was scared. What did a seventeen-year-old country kid know about traveling or being on his own?

When my fellow recruits and I arrived on base and met our company commander, we were told that we were the worst looking bunch of recruits he had ever seen. In fact, he was pretty sure that the United States would fall to the Communists if it were up to us to stop them.

The Marines call them drill instructors, but the Navy calls them company commanders. No matter what you call them, the men and women who control their units and initiate recruits are quite good at yelling.

It felt like everyone at boot camp was smarter than me. Coming from a small town, I was naive about a lot of things. Many of my fellow recruits were much more experienced and came from cities like Chicago, Philadelphia and New York. Their worldliness and sophisticated manner of speaking shook my confidence. And, the more intimidated I felt, the less clearly I seemed to think. I found myself making minor mistakes and having trouble learning.

One day I accidentally stenciled my last name over the wrong pocket of my pants. I was scared to death to walk to the front of the barracks and show the company commander my mistake. There's nothing quite like being berated by the commander in front of your squad. That's when the commander's language, shouted directly into a young recruit's face, tends to be the most colorful. Among other things, he let me know very clearly that I'd gone from being a rock to a bug. Even I was smart enough to recognize I'd been demoted!

But amazingly, I eventually changed from hating my company commander to truly appreciating him. That appreciation came, of course, after boot camp was over. It was only then that I understood why boot camp instructors do what they do. Drill instructors are charged with taking kids from various races, religions and socioeconomic backgrounds and melding them into *one* family. And they have just eight to twelve weeks to do it.

Never in my life have I seen such a diverse group of people come together like we did and learn to genuinely care about one another.

Like it or not, we all hold judgments about people who are different from us, which often creates splits and friction within a group. The military knows that it can't operate successfully if there is this kind of division. That's why drill instructors tear down the men and women who report to boot camp—in order to rebuild them. Over time, individual recruits are no longer considered black or white, Catholic or Protestant. They are flyboys, marines, sailors and soldiers. They are one.

Boot camp taught us the unique culture of the military—its language and its protocols—in order for us to communicate effectively and to function as a team. There was a lot to learn.

For example, recruits bring their own distinctive slang terminologies and regional dialects. It sometimes felt as though I were in a foreign country. At first I had a tough time understanding anyone from Boston, Philadelphia, or New York City—they talked much faster than this Southern boy could listen. I would just smile and nod. But eventually, I was able to pick up on their pace. As we became familiar with the military's style of communication, we began to speak a common language.

At the time, I couldn't understand why everything we did in boot camp had to be so uniform. Each of us had to make our beds using a tight hospital corner. Each of us had to stow our clothes in our lockers in an identical manner. Our shirts had to have crisp creases in the exact same spot and of course, our shoes had to shine, shine, shine.

Over time I came to realize that there's a method to the military's madness. The officers didn't know what kind of personal baggage each of us had brought to boot camp. We'd all been given standardized intelligence tests, and our recruiters did the best job they could to determine whether we were qualified. But let's face it, some recruits aren't cut out for the military.

In the process of shouting orders and insisting on uniformity, our officers learned a great deal about us. If a recruit isn't willing or able to follow the simplest of commands, then the military needs to know that early on. These individuals quickly wash out of the system within the first few weeks of basic training. The government wisely limits its investment in people who aren't designed to be in the military. And that's best for everyone involved, including the recruit.

There are also issues of mental health and self-esteem. Believe it or not, boot camp helps build self-esteem. Those tasks that stress uniformity—making our beds in an expert manner, organizing our lockers in a specific way, getting our shoes shining and our clothes looking crisp—actually helped us recruits feel good about ourselves. And yes, for me those lessons included quickly learning (and never forgetting) the proper pants pocket on which to stencil my name.

It's amazing what discipline does for a person's self confidence. The Navy was also very big on time-management—we could never show up late for anything, and there were no excuses. I continue to rely on the self-discipline I learned in boot camp in my business life today. In fact, I credit it for much of my professional success. I'm known for my time-management skills; I'm not late for others' meetings, and my own meetings begin on time. This is my way of showing my associates that I respect their time.

As I mentioned, recruits come from all walks of life; the military doesn't know what situations and experiences they were exposed to prior to reporting for duty. Did they have good role models? Are they confident in their abilities? In boot camp, the military spends the time necessary to build a recruit's self-esteem. By teaching responsibility and rewarding performance, basic training provides a sense of accomplishment and self-assurance. Believe me—you don't want men and women fighting for our country if they aren't confident in their abilities.

My boot camp experience greatly increased my self-confidence. Once our squad began marching as a unit, it gave me a real sense of pride. And each time I passed an exam or an inspection or received a "well done" from the company commander, it gave me a boost.

Not only did boot camp increase my self-discipline and confidence, it taught me important managerial skills. I didn't know it at the time, but basic training provided me with a great model for how to indoctrinate people successfully into a company. Years later, when I helped to create SellEthics Marketing Group, I made excellent use of my boot camp lessons.

I learned that any time someone new joins our organization, it's vital that they understand the culture of our company and the language we speak. Like any industry or company, we use jargon and terminologies to which a new employee may never have been exposed. Just as I did in the earliest days of boot camp, new personnel may shut down mentally when everything feels strange and unfamiliar. For example, I might tell a new employee that "B2B has saved our organization a substantial amount of money by streamlining our business processes, which has enhanced our cash flow." If the new employee isn't familiar with the term "B2B" (business-to-business applications handled electronically), then the rest of the sentence will probably sound like: "...blah, blah, blah, blah, blah."

I also learned that it's best to find out early if a business "recruit" is going to make it or not. It's important to give a new employee some fairly easy tasks at the beginning, to see if he or she follows directions well. For example, if you told a new employee that you needed a specific report from her on Thursday at 2:00 p.m. and it doesn't arrive by that time, then you likely have a problem. On the other hand, if she does complete the task properly, it gives you an opportunity to provide positive reinforcement for a job well done.

Just like the military, I can never be sure that a job candidate is the right fit until he or she spends time in our company's boot camp. The moment someone joins an organization, it's crucial to set into motion ways to determine if the individual is well-suited to the company.

That way, both the company and the new employee can shine, shine, shine.

Summary

The life lessons to take from this chapter are:

1) For a group to function as a team, it's crucial that there not be divisions between people of various backgrounds. Once a diverse group of individuals becomes committed to working together toward a common goal, trust begins to build between the members.

2) There are many benefits to a disciplined life. Practicing self-discipline helps to build self-confidence. Have you ever known a successful person who doesn't have confidence? The question becomes: Does success breed confidence or does confidence breed success?

3) Anyone who is new to an organization must first be taught the culture of the company. He or she needs to become familiar with policies and procedures, as well as terminology specific to the industry or company. This provides a solid foundation for personal growth and an opportunity for that individual to become a valuable member of the team.

4) New employees should be given opportunities to complete realistic tasks to determine their ability to follow orders. It's important that a company quickly determine whether an individual is going to succeed in that particular environment. Neither the military nor business can afford to waste resources training someone who isn't qualified. On the other hand, if an associate does a good job with tasks early on, providing plenty of positive reinforcement ensures that the candidate will be off to a good start.

Runaway Torpedo

Runaway torpedo: A torpedo that fails to lock on to a designated target and travels aimlessly until it hits an object or runs out of fuel.

After completing boot camp, I was assigned to various training programs. In quartermaster training, I learned to navigate surface ships. From there I traveled to Groton, Connecticut, for submarine school, plus a special submarine navigation school. The schools were challenging, but somehow I made my way through. (Thank goodness for multiple choice tests.)

While I was in training, I was told to fill out a form telling the Navy where I'd like to be stationed after graduation. I was pretty excited about the possibilities, identifying Honolulu, Hawaii, as my first choice, followed by San Diego, California. What I didn't realize is that sailors had a non-official term for this particular government form—the *wish list.*

Wishes didn't come true for me. Instead of Honolulu or San Diego, I ended up in

Charleston, South Carolina, which wasn't even on my list. However, it was in Charleston that I met my future wife, Maggie. But that's a story for another chapter.

In Charleston, I was assigned to the USS Stonewall Jackson, a boomer class submarine with sixteen nuclear warheads. This submarine spent its time hiding in the ocean waiting for the US to launch a nuclear attack. A Blue and a Gold crew took turns taking the submarine out to sea in three-month rotations. When one crew had the boat out to sea, the other crew spent three months in Charleston going through training exercises to prepare for their next time out.

My orders read to report to Chief Edward Bruette, who was in charge of the Jackson's navigation crew. I climbed down the submarine's hatch, and there was Bruette— over six feet tall, with salt and pepper hair and a distinctive goatee. The Chief conveyed an air of professionalism that instantly won my respect. But he had a great smile, too; I soon discovered that he was as friendly as he was professional.

Bruette's uniform was immaculate, and he had a chest full of ribbons for military honors. He also had what every submariner desires—dolphins. Dolphins are an insignia indicating that a sailor is submarine qualified. To receive this emblem, the sailor must know everything about how the submarine operates.

From launching torpedoes to creating power with a nuclear reactor, each submariner had to be knowledgeable about the inner workings of the sub. With such a small crew, we were all interdependent, so each one had to know a little something about every area of the submarine. This way if one of the sailors became incapacitated, someone could easily take over their workstation and keep things going until the issue was resolved. Sailors with dolphins are highly respected not only for their qualifications but also for their ability to handle a lot of stress. Chief Bruette fit that to a tee.

Chief Bruette welcomed me on board and showed me where to stow my duffel bag. He introduced me to the crew and took me on a tour of the submarine. I couldn't have felt more nervous and intimidated. Everyone on board had been in the military for several years, and I was one of only a very few new people assigned to the submarine. But Bruette took a personal interest in me from the start. He had a lot to teach me about submarines, about the Navy and about life. And there was no doubt about it, I had a lot to learn.

My first lesson from the Chief came shortly into my tour of the submarine. It started with his simple question: "Why did you join the Navy?"

I explained that I wanted to get away from my small town.

"Ah," he said, "You're running *away* from something instead of running *towards* something."

I hadn't thought about it that way before. It was true that I didn't have any long-range plans; I just knew that I didn't want to stay where I was.

"You're like a *runaway torpedo*," he continued. "You had three hundred and sixty degrees in either direction around you, so you could have ended up anywhere. How do you know if where you're headed is the right direction?"

It wasn't hard to picture myself as a runaway torpedo: self-propelled, traveling at high speed through the ocean without a target.

Bruette went on: "Some people move away from something, some move towards something, and some just stay locked right where they are, never learning or growing. The good news is, at least you were motivated to move. But it's always better to have an idea of where you're going and why you're going there. You'll appreciate your military experience more if you understand the benefits."

I was moving all right, but I hadn't really thought specifically about what I could get out of this experience in the military. I only knew that it was keeping me from milking cows and shucking corn.

"No matter what job you have, there will always be good days and bad," said the Chief. "If you stay focused on *why* you're doing what you're doing, it'll help you stay motivated even during the difficult times."

Bruette asked me to create a list of good reasons for being in the military. One that came immediately to mind was the Navy's college fund. No one in my family had ever graduated with a four-year degree. The chief also reminded me that the military teaches important communication, leadership, and organizational techniques that could help me succeed in whatever field I decided to pursue in life.

"And you'll find it much easier to get a job in the civilian world," he added. "You'll probably get the nod over someone who hadn't served in the military."

As it turned out, all these benefits reaped great rewards for me. I took advantage of the Navy's educational assistance program, and, after leaving the military, I used the funds to get a bachelor's degree in business. Bruette was absolutely right about the numerous life skills that the military taught me.

He was also right about the importance of taking time to understand and appreciate why I was in the Navy. It offered so much more than just a way to avoid my past. I was able to take the best from the experience. Bruette taught me to focus on the benefits of wherever I may be in the present and to use my experiences to get me where I want to go.

I kept the chief's advice in mind as I graduated from college and began my business career. I kept it in mind as I started a company with four friends of mine. Today, I refuse to live my life like a runaway torpedo, running aimlessly with no target in sight. Instead, I clearly focus on where I am and where I am headed. This has been a valuable tool in my success.

Summary

The life lessons to take from this chapter are:

1) Don't leave your present situation until you've clearly thought through where you're going. Without a sense of direction, you may end up in a worse situation than the one you left.
2) Understand the value of where you are. There are pros and cons to every situation. For example, even a job you dislike probably offers you something to learn and a chance to build your professional skills. It's important to focus on the good in whatever your present situation might be, so that you can stay motivated during difficult times.
3) Things don't always end up like you plan, but that's okay. I ended up in

Charleston, South Carolina, instead of Honolulu, Hawaii. But I can't imagine what my life might be if I hadn't been sent to Charleston and if I hadn't met my wife Maggie. So don't get discouraged if you end up a little off course in life from where you thought you would be. There's no telling what great things might be waiting for you.

Anchors Aweigh

Anchors aweigh: A term used to tell a ship's crew to pull up the anchor and get ready to set sail.

I hate to admit it but I was struggling terribly to become submarine qualified to where I could earn my dolphins. I was dating Maggie at the time, and she would hear from my fellow shipmates that they didn't think I was going to make it. In their opinion, I was just a dumb country boy who couldn't grasp the complex nature of how a submarine operates.

I studied hard, but I was having a tough time getting the material to stick. I wanted so badly to become submarine qualified. My primary reason for wanting to receive my dolphins was that I couldn't stand the disrespect I was receiving from not being submarine qualified. When you get your dolphins, you become part of a fraternity of sailors. Until then, you are an outsider with no value to anyone. The abuse was practically non-stop. If there was a dirty job to do (like kitchen duty), I had to do it because I didn't have my dolphins. If someone wanted my seat, they could take it because I didn't have my dolphins. It was pretty much non-stop hazing. The only way I could get it to stop was to pass all of my submarine qualifications. The qualifications involved constant testing and I was not doing well with them.

Chief Bruette became concerned that I was falling behind, and he asked me what was wrong. I told him that I was afraid I would never get qualified. I was just a country boy who knew nothing accept how to take care of animals. How he responded to the situation completely changed my life.

First, he said that he couldn't believe that I was struggling because he thought that I was very smart. He was proud of the way that I absorbed all of the navigational material and was moving quickly through those particular qualifications. That is when he looked at me and said: "You already have an 85% chance of being very successful at anything you do, including becoming submarine qualified."

I wasn't used to such positive feedback so I was definitely listening intently.

He continued, "The only reason you aren't picking up on the technical side of what you are learning is that you don't have confidence in yourself. When people don't believe in themselves, they create a mental block, which makes it extremely difficult for them to learn. There is no doubt in my mind that you could easily learn how the submarine operates and how to navigate it, but my believing it doesn't matter—you must believe it for yourself. Your doubt is like an anchor tied around your neck.

"Think of your life like this boat. This boat wasn't built to be tied to a pier; it was built to travel from one destination to the next. Your life wasn't meant to be tied down either. You were built to learn, grow, and experience life. Doubt is one of the primary reasons why people never grow. Doubt keeps us tied down and unable to move."

My problem was that I thought everyone was smarter than me when that wasn't the case. I came to realize the only difference between them and me were the experiences we had. How was I supposed to know about something that I had never experienced? It wasn't that I couldn't learn it; I just hadn't seen it before. When I reflected back to my life on the farm, there wasn't anything my father tried to teach me or anything in school that my teachers tried to teach me that I couldn't learn. There were some things that took a little more practice, but I could do anything that I was taught to do.

For some reason, I had blocked out my past successes and instead convinced myself that I wasn't good enough. My chief made it his personal mission to help me gain confidence in myself. As a matter of fact, he was so confident in my ability to learn that he told me that he was going to make me one of the youngest primary navigators on nuclear submarines in U.S. history. A primary navigator is the one who takes over navigating the submarine any time the sub is in dangerous waters, such as when traveling up and down rivers. I was amazed that this man, who was so well respected by everyone, was telling me that he had all this confidence in me. That statement alone completely changed my life. All of a sudden the mental block that I had in place was completely removed, and I started absorbing everything around me. No longer did I have trouble getting qualified at anything.

I feel so sorry for the millions of people who never had someone like Chief Bruette in their lives to tell them there is nothing they can't do. Because once I believed that I could do anything I set my mind to, I could. Not only did I become submarine qualified and received my dolphins, but I also became one of the youngest primary navigators on submarines in U.S. history.

It sounds so simple, but as I mentioned in the introduction, doubt crushes dreams and holds people back personally as well as professionally. So if you get anything at all out of this book, I hope you realize the importance of having confidence in yourself. It is that simple. You can either stay tied to the pier, or you can remove the doubt, cast away the lines that have been holding you back, and get your vessel underway. Anchors aweigh!

Summary

The greatest lessons to learn from this chapter are:

1) Don't ever think that you aren't capable of great things. There is no doubt that we have different aptitudes, experiences, and personalities, which make some things easier to accomplish than others. If you want to have a great life, you have got to get rid of any negative thoughts regarding your abilities.

2) Chief Bruette helped me to get rid of the negative thoughts that were holding me back. You have got to find friends who are encouragers not discouragers. If there are people in your life who bring you down, do what you can to stay away from them.

3) Remind yourself of past accomplishments. It's easy to get caught up in negative thoughts. A great way to remain positive and remind yourself that you are capable of great things is to reflect upon past victories. Once I realized that there wasn't anything

in my past experiences to suggest that I couldn't learn, my whole world changed. The mental block was lifted, and I became a learning machine.

Casting Off

Casting off: A term used to order the crew on top of the ship's deck to untie the lines (ropes) that keep the ship tied to the pier.

If your life were like a ship, how would you describe where it is right now? Is it tied down or are you out making the most of your life and experiencing everything it has to offer?

The greatest problem most people have is that they keep themselves tied to the pier. They allow the lines/ropes of life to prevent them from venturing out and experiencing new things. It would be one thing if people were happy being tied down and unable to move, but a lot of them aren't. People who have a need to achieve or at least have a sense for adventure aren't going to be happy with staying in port. They have got to get out and make things happen. But there are some people who are content remaining tied to the pier. They might not end up successful, at least as Webster's defines it, but they are perfectly happy watching others come and go as they venture out to sea.

I will assume that if you are reading this book, you are not the type of person who likes to sit back and watch the world go by. More than likely you are a bit like me and want to pursue personal and professional growth. So what holds us back? Even when we have a desire to take off and pursue various goals, what keeps us tied to the pier?

I've already shared with you one of the major things that keeps us tied down: *doubt*. When we doubt ourselves we don't have the trust that allows us to let go of the lines and venture out. Confidence in ourselves and our abilities is crucial for experiencing success. This is why most great achievers have strong self-esteem. Have you ever seen that funny picture of a cute kitten looking into a mirror and the reflection in the mirror is of a large lion? It is a fantastic example of great self-esteem. There is always a fine line and some people go overboard with their ego, but the fact of the matter is, in order to achieve you must first believe.

Another major reason that some people never make it out of port is they allow excuses to keep them tied to the pier. I should know, since I grew up using the excuse that I couldn't accomplish anything because I was a poor country boy. I used my lack of experiences and book knowledge as an excuse for not trying hard enough to achieve. Chief Bruette helped me get rid of that excuse once and for all when he told me that I could accomplish anything. Knowing that somebody I respected saw something special in me allowed me to cast off that line that had been keeping me from experiencing success.

This is why it is so difficult for someone who grows up under difficult circumstances (i.e., inner city, rural poverty, etc.) to pull themselves out of that environment. On the other hand, someone who grows up seeing successful people all around him or her has a completely different set of expectations about life. It is truly that simple. How people see themselves and their expectations about life directly impacts where they end up. Life is like any work of art—you must see it in your mind before it ever makes its way onto life's canvass.

Another excuse that some people use is blaming their parents for their own failures and shortcomings. We all experience downtimes at one point or another, but we can hold no other person responsible but ourselves for the results and consequences.

What we are experiencing today is usually a direct result of choices we made in our past. The problem with blaming our parents is that we teach our children to do the same thing. It makes it difficult for them to ever own up and take responsibility for their own set of circumstances. Of course, you can love your children and provide them with wise guidance, but you are not and will not be the sole determinant for what they make of themselves and their lives, just as our parents are not responsible for what we are going through right now.

My parents weren't perfect, but I took good things they taught me and used them to my advantage. I have also learned from their mistakes so that I wouldn't repeat them. Their experiences both good and bad have helped guide me to where I am today.

I need to make this point perfectly clear: You will not experience happiness and/or success in your life until you assume total responsibility for it. The blaming cycle has to end. You will never get out of port if you allow excuses to keep you tied to the pier.

So if you are guilty of blaming others (i.e., how you were raised, lack of education, your spouse and children, etc.) for your not achieving what you want out of life, cast off this line that has been holding you back and set sail for a great adventure.

Summary

The greatest lessons to learn from this chapter are:

1) Doubt is a major factor that holds people back from experiencing a great life.
2) Excuses prevent people from achieving personal and professional goals because they remain tied down, never quite able to reach far enough to experience success.
3) People don't achieve success by accident. They have good self-esteem, and they expect great things. As Zig Ziglar once said: "Whether you believe you can or you believe you can't, you are right."

Point Bravo

Point Bravo: the destination point of the submarine or ship; the opposite of Point Alpha, the place of origin.

My chief was always in a teaching mode.

Top secret orders for the USS Stonewall Jackson arrived regularly, informing us where the sub needed to patrol. After the captain reviewed them, he'd assign a crew member to chart a course to our newest destination.

Bruette looked at me with a serious expression one afternoon and instructed me to chart a course. I jumped up and quickly grabbed my divider, a pencil, and a protractor—the tools I'd need for charting. But just as quickly, I realized that I had one small problem.

"Where are we going?" I asked him.

He smiled, and said, "Ah, that's always the burning question, isn't it?"

I detected another life lesson coming my way—and I was right.

"The problem with most people is that they don't know where they're going," said Bruette.

"Don't ever forget that navigating a vessel is like life. It starts with having a destination in mind."

When navigating the submarine, we were constantly going from Point A to Point B—or from Point Alpha to Point Bravo in military parlance. The radio call signals adopted by the armed forces designate a specific name for every letter of the alphabet. We were always on top secret missions and never named our location, for obvious reasons. If the enemy intercepted a message, they wouldn't know where Point Alpha and Point Bravo were. If we said something like, let's meet by St. Croix and then we will proceed to the island of Granada, the enemy would find it pretty easy to track us down.

As a navigator, I charted a course by knowing exactly where we were (taking a fix), where we were going (our Point Bravo) and what time we were supposed to get there. I ran a straight line from Point A to Point B to determine if there were obstacles preventing us from taking a straight shot to our destination.

Often there were. But by locking in our destination and strategically plotting our course, we were in control of the situation. For instance, when traveling up and down the winding St. Mary's River in King's Bay, Georgia, our charts let us navigate through the various water depths and fluctuations without running aground. We wouldn't have dreamed of letting the river itself dictate where we ended up.

But how often do we allow the rivers of life to control our personal or professional journeys? So many of us tend to be *wish*-oriented rather than *goal*-oriented. We simply wish for what we want, rather than create a plan that will make it happen.

Goals can mean the difference between success and failure. A goal can be likened to Point Bravo. Pinpointing Point Bravo early in your journey provides you with a vital piece of information. Successful people know where they are going and keep themselves focused on the destination. And in general, people are happier having a sense of control over their own destinies.

As a navigator on the Jackson, I would clearly establish a Point Bravo before I charted a course for the submarine. These days, having learned from my Navy experiences, I establish goals that help me chart a course for my life. And I do it on paper.

I highly recommend writing down your goals. In fact, I write a fresh set of them each year. Some I've achieved, while others are still works in progress. By having my goals in writing, it's easy to see how they've changed over time. That's a pretty good indication that I've changed as well. Some of my earlier goals seem pretty silly to me years later, but I guess that proves I'm maturing.

Your Point Bravo could be completely different from my Point Bravo. One person might love to travel to Italy, while another may aspire to travel across the United States in a motor home. One company employee may want to be the national vice-president of sales; another thinks it would be great to head the human resources department.

Goals keep us motivated and striving for the best possible outcomes. Without goals, we risk running aground or settling for less.

When setting a goal, it's important to know *why* you've chosen it. Be wary of goals that conflict with your core values. For example, if you want to have more time for yourself and your family, then aspiring to upper-level management may not be right for you. The hours necessary to achieve this goal would directly conflict with personal and family time. So ask yourself: "*Why* do I want this goal?" and "Will it require sacrifices that I am willing to make?" Only you can answer these important questions.

Successful people don't end up where they are by chance; they create goals for themselves and pursue them with passion. When they achieve one goal, they move on to the next. Successful people realize the power of goal setting and the tremendous motivation and joy that charting their dreams provides.

Do you have vague wishes or do you have specific goals? Remember, every successful journey begins with a clear destination!

Summary

The life lessons to take from this chapter are:

1) Don't try to navigate through life without designating a Point Bravo. To enjoy life to its fullest and to experience personal, professional and spiritual growth, it's critical to establish annual goals. But writing goals doesn't have to be complicated; check out my example of goal setting on the next page.

2) Ask yourself "Why is this particular goal important to me?" and "Are my goals consistent with my core values?" Be brutally honest with yourself. Carefully think through why you want certain goals. And be sure that once you achieve your goals, the lives of you and your loved ones actually will be improved.

3) Successful people know that they didn't make it there by chance. They had a vision and a clear idea about how to achieve it.

4) It's entirely up to you; you can continue to float down the river of life, allowing it to take you wherever it leads (and I promise, you'll always have plenty of company), or you can choose your own destination points along the way. It is truly that simple.

ANNUAL GOALS

1) *To spend more time with my children.* I promise to create one night a month which will be designated as game night.
2) *To be a better husband for my wife.* I promise to take her out on a special date night once every two weeks.
3) *To enhance my faith.* I promise to not miss church unless I or someone in the household is sick or if I am traveling.
4) *To not be such a workaholic.* I promise to do everything in my power to make it home by 6:00 every night.
5) *To relax more.* I promise to read six recreational books this year.

Set and Drift

Set and drift: Characteristics of a current, including the velocity of the water in which a ship is sailing. Set is the direction the current is moving, while drift is the speed of the current, usually measured in knots. The direction and speed of a current can easily take a navigator off course.

On the USS Stonewall Jackson, we limited the number of times we'd approach the surface to determine our precise position or in Navy terms, take a navigational fix. That's because we were always on top secret missions – we didn't want to be spotted by either enemies or friendlies. Our primary mission was to hide from everyone for three months.

Navigating a submarine can be quiet and uneventful when it's traveling in the middle of the ocean, with no dangerous obstacles for hundreds of miles. We'd take the sub up close to the surface and I'd obtain a satellite fix by sending up an antenna to get the latitude and longitude reading. I'd plot the readings on my chart and continue to track any speed or course changes. Such changes would affect where we were on the chart; we couldn't risk getting off track. Periodically, the officer of the deck authorized going up for another fix to verify our position. It was a fine art – I loved it when my projections and the actual fix were right on top of one another.

Navigating up and down rivers was completely different – there was much more noise and excitement. Winding rivers mean numerous course corrections and speed changes. We made sure to take frequent fixes on our location.

The officer of the deck was usually stationed on top of the submarine in the sailplane. A couple of lookouts were there too. Chief Bruette manned the periscope and was constantly watching, ready to take a round of bearings on various navigational aids. He provided me current bearings based upon landmarks such as church towers, lighthouses and radio towers. About every two or three minutes, he would give me a very fast sequence: St. Phillips Steeple – bearing mark 138.7 degrees; Northeast radio tower – bearing mark 24.7 degrees; Morris Island Lighthouse – bearing mark 247.3 degrees.

Each time he called out a bearing, I'd set my protractor to the degrees he called out and run the arm of my protractor from the river to the mark indicating the proper landmark on the chart. Three bearings from Chief Bruette meant three lines drawn on my chart – our sub was at the point where these lines intersected. I quickly evaluated our course and speed and let the officer of the deck know if we needed to make any changes to either. I then drew our course on the chart and taking speed into consideration, I identified exactly where we'd be three minutes from our present fix, as well as six minutes out. We never knew if something might happen that would prohibit us from taking another round of bearings in three minutes.

Communication typically went from me to the Captain. The Captain would then tell the chief on duty to make the recommended course and/or speed change. There was usually an officer or a chief giving directions to the helmsman and the engine room. Everyone was on alert to make necessary changes in speed and course corrections. There were a lot of things happening within those three minute intervals and I really had to think fast. Sometimes it got very loud, but I tuned out everything except for what I needed to hear to do my job.

Nobody wanted the submarine to run aground. This happened to some crews; running aground necessitated waiting for the authorities (senior commanders) to arrive and assess the situation. They'd then take control of the submarine and make sure that it got in safely. At that point, the captain of the submarine, the navigator (the leading officer in charge of the navigation department), the officer of the deck (the one in charge of the submarine at the time of the accident, usually the captain), the harbor pilot (if there was one appointed), and the primary navigator would be questioned thoroughly to determine what happened and who was at fault. Ultimately, the captain paid the price, no matter what his crew might have done.

I learned very early on that to successfully navigate a submarine, I had to pay very close attention to set and drift. The speed and direction of a current can get a navigator off course from where he's expected to be.

The concept of set and drift also relates to life. No matter what direction you think your life is headed in, at some point you'll inevitably be taken off course. Life flows in currents – and much of its movement is out of our control. The world around us is always changing, which means we need to make regular personal and professional course corrections. For example, a company may discover that the very same strategy that made it successful initially may not be effective later on. No matter how carefully we plan, life exerts a force all its own.

Knowing that our submarine would be negatively affected by set and drift, we made sure to take frequent fixes on our location. We did this by using navigational satellites and by using navigational aids or landmark indicators. We took frequent fixes so that we could make regular course corrections.

Most people fail to take fixes on where they are in life. Instead, they let set and drift determine their life direction. Successful people know that they can't allow this to happen. They establish goals and identify measurable "fixes" along the way to determine if they are on the right course. If they discover that they are off-course, successful people immediately make the necessary corrections.

For example, some people sit around and wait to be hand-picked by upper-management to move up into the ranks, while others purposefully position themselves for advancement. I did the latter throughout my career. I learned this tactic in the military – I established specific goals that guaranteed a promotion in rank. I took this plan with me when I entered the regular workforce and it has propelled me time and time again to the next level.

I can't think of any tool that's been more instrumental to my success more than the personal development plan. Here's how it works. First, you identify the attributes, knowledge, and skills necessary for the position that you're interested in. One way to do this is to obtain the job description and requirements for the position you want.

Another way (my favorite) is to ask your boss for input. This lets your boss know that you're interested in moving up the ladder while giving you an opportunity to keep him or her posted on your progress.

It's amazing how many people aren't promoted because they simply don't let anyone know they're interested in moving up. And then they're upset when they aren't chosen. Being ambitious means nothing if you're the only one who knows it!

Creating a personal development plan is easy (Appendix A). Assigning specific dates helps to keep you focused on where you're headed so that life circumstances – set and drift – don't take you off course. If they do, don't beat yourself up – just allow sufficient time to adjust and to get back on course.

You can merely cross your fingers and hope for your next promotion or you take control of your course – it's that simple. Just imagine the positive reaction you'd receive from your boss if you shared your success in achieving personal goals. If I were your boss, I'd make sure you were on the fast track!

Another great technique for establishing a personal fix is 360 degree review (Appendix B). Many companies use this tool to determine how business associates perceive a particular worker in terms of his or her skill areas, such as communication and industry knowledge.

Have you ever worked with an individual who held an opinion of himself that was completely different from everyone else's view? A 360 degree review is intended to help individuals see themselves as others see them. This reality check can be difficult, but, you won't be effective until you understand how you fit into the bigger picture.

To successfully navigate your life, you must know where you are and where you are going. This requires concrete information. A personal development plan and a 360 degree review provide specific insights that will allow you to make the course adjustments necessary to achieve your goals.

Create a plan (chart a course), measure where you are (take a fix), and then adjust accordingly. Don't let the *set* and *drift* of life get in the way of accomplishing great things. While others idly glide along with the wayward currents, you'll be navigating your way to a fantastic life!

Summary:

The life lessons to take from this chapter are:

1) Set and drift are facts of life – and so is the need to make regular course corrections. Because the world is

       constantly changing, it's necessary to take frequent fixes on where we are and where we're headed.

2) To stay on course and accomplish your goals, develop a Personal Development Plan. "Reference my example at the end of this chapter."

3) Sometimes there's a difference between how we see ourselves and how others see us. The 360 degree review is a helpful tool in adjusting your course and accomplishing your goals. "Reference my example at the end of this chapter."

PERSONAL DEVELOPMENT PLAN

January 1 – December 31

Goal #1:

To be considered extremely knowledgeable in such areas as leadership principles, purchase decisions, promotional vehicles, competitive activity, and area customers.

Plan of Action:

- Attend one leadership seminar by February 28th.
- Meet with research and development to discuss consumer trends and product attributes on all major brands. Make sure everyone in our department has a copy of my findings by April 30th.

- Meet with marketing to discuss the most cost-effective promotional vehicles for building market share by May 28th.
- Create a list of all major competitors and identify their strengths and weaknesses. Make sure everyone in our department has a copy of my findings by September 30th.
- Read two books on leadership and do a two-page book report on each listing what I have learned and how I will apply the principles. I'll have the reports to our sales manager by December 31st.

Goal #2:

To be considered an extremely effective presenter by my peers and key management.

Plan of Action:

- Take a course on effective presentation techniques by June 1st.
- Take an advanced course in PowerPoint and share the highlights of what I learned with the department by October 31st.

360 DEGREE REVIEW (CONFIDENTIAL)

Name: Betty Thompson
Date: January 15th
Score: 1 = Strongly Agree
               2 = Agree   3 = Mildly
               Agree 4 = Disagree

Note: 1.) Please provide a comment for any score that is 3 or less 2.) If you do not feel you can rate a particular area, please put a 0 down for the score 3.) Feel free to score in fractions (i.e. 2.5 for knowledge, 1.3 for organization, etc.).

1. Betty is perceived to be very professional in dealing with people.
2. Betty is an effective communicator via the phone/voicemail.
3. Betty is an effective communicator via email.
4. Betty is a great team player (i.e. helpful, enthusiastic, positive, etc.).
5. Betty is a good listener.

6. Betty is good at following up on requests/issues.

7. Betty treats people with respect and appreciation.

8. Betty is knowledgeable about her areas of responsibility.

9. Betty has great technology skills (i.e. Excel, PowerPoint, Word, etc.)

10. I am proud that Betty is a member of our team.

Comments (optional):

Charts

Charts: Special maps used by navigators to plot where they are and where they are going. Charts provide specific types of information, such as water depth and underwater topography, so that the navigator knows where it is safe to travel. They also list lighthouses and church towers, so if navigators see these landmarks, they can position themselves and determine if they are headed in the right direction. Accurate charts are critical for the safe navigation of a ship.

The USS Stonewall Jackson patrolled the Atlantic Ocean, which encompasses more than forty-one million square miles. This is about twenty percent of the earth's surface. To put it into perspective, our territory was about twelve times the size of the United States.

Since we had nuclear warheads on board, our missions were top secret. Most of our crew didn't know where we were going; only specific departments had the need to know.

Imagine traveling under the ocean for three months, with no idea where you are or what's going on outside. Three months of no sunrises or sunsets. Three months of working seven days a week, barely able to keep track of what day it is. It takes a certain breed of sailor to handle this type of environment.

The ocean is a dangerous place for a submarine because it's filled with mountain ranges and volcanoes. My job as a quartermaster was to ensure that our sub avoided these hazards and that the USS Stonewall Jackson and its crew moved safely from one destination to the next. Not an easy task when there are no windows. It's pretty much like driving a car while wearing a blindfold.

Chief Bruette taught me everything I know about safely navigating a submarine up and down rivers and across the ocean. He consistently stressed the importance of maintaining our charts. Charts are to water what maps are to land. Instead of cities, highways and exits, navigational charts are marked with buoys, latitude and longitude lines, water depths, etc.

"Charts are the combined experiences of sailors who traveled the ocean before us," Bruette always reminded us. "Treat them with respect."

When early ocean adventurers encountered land, they would document their discoveries so that others taking the same journey would know what to expect. When sailing in uncharted waters, early ships were likely to run aground on a shelf that they couldn't see. Often these ships would break apart and the sailors would jump overboard, hoping to be rescued by a sister ship. These sailors would then document their experiences, enabling future navigators to learn from their misfortune.

It would be foolish to attempt to navigate around the ocean without the wisdom of the early sailors. In teaching me to respect our charts, Chief taught me to value and appreciate the wisdom of these sailors. But that's not all— he also taught me to value and appreciate the wisdom of people who have gone before me in any of life's journeys.

Ever since those days on the submarine, I've paid special attention to my elders' stories— tales of their successes and of their failures. Taking note of their experiences, I've been able to avoid a lot of hazards in my own life. I've also been able to make sound choices about career moves and finances, thanks to words of wisdom from people I respect.

It seems to me that most other cultures respect elders more than we do in the United States. For some reason, Americans often choose to go it alone, rather than tap into the wisdom that is so readily available. Maybe it's seen as a sign of weakness to need counsel from others. But why should generation after generation be forced to run aground and make the same mistakes?

Chief Bruette held enormous respect for the experiences of other sailors. Using him as a role model, I am a life-long learner—someone who appreciates and benefits from the experiences of others. I'm hungry for knowledge, whether it comes from books, conversation, or classes. When it comes to making the best choices in my life, I don't hesitate to seek counsel. I have had a fantastic life, and it hasn't been by accident. There are so many people whose wisdom and guidance I respect. I've learned from the experiences of people like Anthony Robbins, Brian Tracy, Jim Rohn, Dr. Stephen Covey, and Zig Ziglar, to name a few.

Just as charts help a navigator safely travel the ocean, the life experiences of our elders can help us safely navigate the journey of life. Why risk running aground? Why risk ending up somewhere where you don't want to be? Tap into the experiences of those around you so you can make wise choices in your own life.

Summary

The life lessons to take from this chapter are:

1) Once you know your destination, you need to find the charts necessary to get there. These charts are the experiences—

both positive and negative—of others on a similar journey. Their wisdom will make your journey much smoother.

2) Don't consider it a sign of weakness to solicit advice from others. The greatest leaders of all time surrounded themselves with talented people and tapped into their collective knowledge and wisdom.

3) Respect your elders. These experienced people have great stories to share. Visit a nursing home or take an elderly relative out for lunch and ask him or her for advice. (For example: What do you think is the secret to success? How do you keep a marriage strong? If you could do anything over again, what would you do differently? What's the best decision you ever made?) Not only will you gain tremendous wisdom, but they will feel appreciated and needed. This is a real "win-win" situation.

Watertight Integrity

Watertight integrity: the Navy standard that ensures a vessel is sound and that water cannot penetrate the hull of the ship. Without watertight integrity, a ship risks sinking.

It's no exaggeration to say that the lives of the submarine's crew members depended upon the watertight integrity of the USS Stonewall Jackson.

The hull of the vessel was made of titanium steel and carefully designed to withstand enormous water pressure. If you've ever dived under water, you understand water pressure; just going ten feet down can make your ears hurt. In the ocean, the water pressure at ten feet is the equivalent of six hundred and forty pounds pressing on your body. Now imagine going down to a depth of one hundred, or even one thousand feet!

Unlike other ships, which only need to worry about water penetrating a portion of their hulls, our entire submarine was submerged and exposed to water pressure. Leaks could occur anywhere, so our crew had to put the submarine's integrity to the test on a regular basis.

I learned this the first time I went out to sea and was told that we were taking the sub down to test depth. "What's test depth?" I asked my Chief.

He explained that each submarine is given a rating—based on factors such as age—to indicate the depth that it can reach before the boat begins to form leaks.

"Before we begin our patrol," Bruette said, "we have to test this boat to make sure it can withstand that kind of pressure. We need to know our range of operation before we go into a hide mode at sea. Then we'll know how deep we can go before we run into trouble."

Other crew members, each of them wearing a headphone, were to be assigned to various stations in the submarine. Bruette explained that we would then proceed to test depth. "And they'll let us know when the water pressure starts popping rivets out of the wall."

He couldn't be serious. "You mean to tell me, "I asked in disbelief, "that we go deep enough that stuff starts popping off the wall?"

"Oh, yes," said Bruette calmly, "we'll start seeing minor leaks. Sometimes even major ones, if we don't catch them in time. That's why you went through damage control training in submarine school, so that you'd know how to fix holes that burst."

At that moment, I questioned my decision to join the submarine force. But I soon realized that this depth test—like so many other Navy drills and inspections—was about maintaining the highest standards possible. It was about reliability and integrity—the integrity of the submariners who ensure the integrity of their vessel.

Integrity—it's a good foundation, not only for submarine operations, but for life.

Why is integrity so important? Let's talk about the issue of trust. On the Jackson, we trusted the integrity of our fellow crew members with our lives. How can any relationship, whether personal or professional, succeed without trust?

And remember, little leaks can compromise water-tightness, just as bigger leaks can. Likewise, if you can't trust someone's decisions about little things, then why would you trust their decisions on the bigger issues?

Trust is hard to earn and easily lost. Just as our submarine's hull experienced incredible water pressure, people often experience incredible societal pressures that can damage their integrity. The problem with watertight integrity is that you either have it or you don't. Even a small hole in our sub could have taken us to the bottom of the ocean. Our integrity isn't watertight if we compromise our value system, even if it's just a little bit here and there. We can still sink.

I like to use the following litmus test to gauge my actions: If all the things that I say and do were printed in the newspaper, would I be okay with it? And when they read about my actions, would my family be proud of me, or ashamed?

People don't typically rupture a major leak. Over time, they tend to pop minor ones here and there. Sometimes we're able to get away with little transgressions along the way, but it only ends up setting us up for a big fall.

Have you ever told a little white lie? Maybe you just allowed someone to believe something when you knew it wasn't true. This can be tempting in business when, for example, you're trying to bring on a new client. Let's say that the client thinks you can turn a project around in two weeks, even though you know it will probably take four. But revealing that might cost you the job, so you don't say anything.

Your boss may be happy that you landed the project, but the customer won't be happy when his expectations aren't met. Now let's suppose you get away with it. You pull out the charm and calm down the client when he complains. Still, there's a pretty good chance that he'll tell other potential clients about his bad experience. You may not feel the pinch on your sales today, but what about down the road, when you've developed a reputation of not delivering to customers' expectations?

When we compromise our personal or professional integrity, it never turns out well. Somehow we always seem to get caught. The Bible says it best: "The man of integrity walks securely, but he who takes crooked paths will be found out" *(Proverbs 12:22)*.

Which brings me to why, in 1999, four of my friends and I decided to form our own food brokerage company—SellEthics Marketing Group, Inc. The word "Ethics" is in our name not just to tell the world how we do business, but to remind ourselves each day that we must live up to our name. Believe me, there have been many times that we've been tempted to bend the truth to get ahead or to get out of a tight spot. But in the end, we remember our commitment to ethics and to doing the right thing, no matter what the consequences. Over the years, we have never regretted telling the truth. Don't get me wrong—it can hurt to admit to a client that you messed up. But in the end, it usually improves your relationship.

Sometimes we get the idea in our heads that our customers think we'll be perfect. But in reality, they don't expect us to be perfect. They just expect that when we do mess up, we'll do everything in our power to make it right.

Here's the truth: even if we never get caught in a lie, there's a problem. Whenever we compromise our integrity, a piece of us is lost. The resulting guilt takes away our joy. And it's hard to have effective relationships when we don't feel good about ourselves. Our self-esteem directly impacts all of our relationships.

Having watertight integrity is critical to experiencing a life of happiness and success. Just like on a submarine, there will always be pressures that put our water-tightness to the test. But there's no room for compromise when it comes to your value system. Maintain those high standards of conduct for yourself—and keep your life afloat.

Summary

The greatest lessons to learn from this chapter are:

1) Watertight integrity is critical to having a great life. It affects all of our relationships in one way or another.
2) Integrity doesn't come in degrees—you either have it or you don't.
3) Small compromises in integrity are like small leaks. They can still sink a ship!

Sea Worthy

Sea worthy: A term used to describe whether a vessel is in good enough shape to survive a trip at sea.

Could you imagine going out to sea and not being sure whether your vessel could handle the trip? Our submarine not only had to be able to float on the surface, but it also had to have the ability to go under the water without springing leaks and sinking to the bottom.

The crew on the USS Stonewall Jackson had it drilled into our heads to take great care of our boat. I had never thought about it before, but Chief Bruette explained to me that throughout the ages, captains have referred to their vessel in the female gender. The reason for this, he explained, is that the crew would take better care of the ship if they thought of it as a woman. It may sound crazy, but it worked. Sailors more naturally paid attention to the vessel and made sure she was well taken care of due to the image the captain created.

Being seaworthy entailed many critical components when it came to the Jackson. First, the executive officers had to make sure they had enough qualified personnel to operate the sub successfully while at sea. New personnel were often assigned to the crew, and not all of them had the qualifications necessary to man a watch. With this in mind, the captain needed to know if his crew could handle the work shifts while the new crew member got up to speed on his particular work station.

The department heads (leading officers) also had to go through a checklist to ensure all applicable equipment was in working order and that back-up supplies were available to keep the equipment running for several months.

The captain would also have the outside of the hull inspected, including the section under water. Navy Seals were typically used to dive under the sub and check for problems.

The supply officer had a very important role on the submarine because he had to make sure we had everything we needed (i.e., back-up parts, food, etc.) so we could stay out for several months without needing to stop anywhere. Failure to do so would negatively affect our mission to stay undetected during our patrol. Careers were often made or destroyed for any officer taking on this particular assignment. It required unbelievable organizational skills.

Lastly, the captain had to make sure the outside of the hull was protected from the potential damage of salt water, so the deck crew had to chip paint, remove rust, and reapply a fresh coat of special paint that helped maintain the ship's watertight integrity.

The crew also required a lot of preparation. It can be likened to someone going out of town for an extended period. For those of us who weren't married, we had to make sure to pay all applicable bills up front (i.e., car loan, apartment rent, utilities, etc.) and that our mail was held. The Navy did help us out by giving us our money up front so that we could take care of things before going on patrol. For sailors who lived on base, this windfall of money before heading out to sea often provided them with an opportunity to blow it before even leaving port. (Of course, that is what helped keep the local economy going.)

One thing that I always found funny when going on patrol is that at least one guy always figured he would use the opportunity while out at sea with no grocery store available to quit smoking. This often did not go well. What would inevitably happen is that the individual would pay a lot of money for cigarettes from one of his crewmates. There were actually a few entrepreneurs (one I knew who didn't even smoke) who brought extra smokes on board for anyone unable to quit. Of course, there was a pretty significant mark-up for the cigarettes—

I believe economists call this a "convenience utility."

Once again this nautical concept can be applied to life. Are you seaworthy? Once you have decided upon a goal/destination for your life, you have to figure out whether you are ready for the journey. Too many people make the mistake of not thinking through this critical component and find themselves over their head as they take on certain goals.

One example of this is your education. There are always exceptions to the rule but let's face it, having a successful career is much easier when you have a college education. Having a college degree opens up doors for you that would not otherwise be available. Did you know that a majority of prison inmates are high school dropouts? Who knows what a kid might be thinking at the time, but an individual who drops out of school severely diminishes their chances for having a good life.

As I mentioned earlier, I'm the first one in my family to earn a four-year degree. My siblings are successful, but they had to work hard to get to where they are today. They also missed out on various opportunities along the way because they did not have a college degree. Fortunately for them, the lessons they learned growing up regarding hard work and dedication have served them well over the years.

Whatever adventure you decide to pursue, you must make sure you have the tools necessary to accomplish the journey. For example if you want to be a public speaker, then you should take the courses necessary at your local college to hone those skills. If you want to be a writer, then take writing courses. If you want to change careers and do something in the IT/IS field, then you should find out what courses you need to acquire various certifications. It is important that you don't just take off without first doing your homework. Your homework should include talking to someone who is in the field that you are pursuing in order to receive advice about how best to go about acquiring the skills and positioning yourself for a career.

I appreciate the fact that some people are risk takers and they go out and try different things. Even if they fail, they at least learn from the experience. The problem is that they often end up crashing and burning because they didn't prepare like they should. If you are going to try something, why not put yourself in the best position for making it happen?

Making sure you are seaworthy is a critical component to success. You can either waste a lot of years trying and failing at different things, or you can do it right the first time by doing your homework and making sure you have all the tools necessary for a smooth voyage.

Summary

The greatest lessons to learn from this chapter are:

1) Most people fail in their efforts to pursue a goal due to a lack of preparation.

2) Make sure when you assign yourself a goal that you do the necessary homework to ensure you have thought through everything that it will take (i.e., aptitude, certifications, degree resources, skills, training, etc.) so that you will have the best shot possible of achieving your objective.

3) Seek counsel from other people who have accomplished what you are attempting to do. They can help you think through all of the various elements that will be involved in your journey.

4) At least try! I hope that you pursue your dreams via preparation, but even if you don't—go for it! You don't want to find yourself years down the road wondering "what if?" Trying and failing are much better on your psyche than beating yourself up for never trying in the first place.

General Quarters

General Quarters: An announcement made over the intercom system that lets everyone know they must report to battle stations.

I believe the military does a lot of things right, and one of the most successful things they do is communicate. They know when to handle something via email, voicemail, or in person. Based upon the message, the means in which you communicate should change in order to enhance its effectiveness so it is understood thoroughly.

As a sailor, when you heard the *general quarters alarm* you knew something important was going on. Everyone would run to their battle stations and wait to hear what the issue was. My job during these times was to take over as primary plotter. This assignment entailed trying to figure out the point of origin for an enemy torpedo so that we could perform evasive maneuvers.

Once everyone got to their battle stations (which only took a couple of minutes), the captain would then use the intercom to let everyone know what was going on. Some times it was a practice drill, while other times it was the real deal.

I'll never forget the time when I was woken up around two in the morning by the general quarters alarm. I could already tell that it was some type of avoidance maneuver as I felt the submarine go into a dive, which made getting dressed a little more challenging. I ran to my station expecting to hear the captain say that it was only a drill. When I arrived in the control room, the captain had a very serious look on his face and the whole room had a different feel about it. He then went on to announce that there was a torpedo in the water heading straight towards us.

I admit that my heart rate went up a little bit, but then I also noticed that I was subconsciously already preparing my workstation so that I could figure out the direction the torpedo was traveling. All of those practice drills had paid off as everyone around the room had a calm, professional demeanor about them.

Most torpedoes are pretty good at figuring out where the target is. The torpedo emits a fairly broad underwater signal and then listens for the sound wave to bounce off of something. Once it acquires its target, it can be difficult to shake. That's what we found with this one. It just kept coming. I can't go into all of the things we did to shake this torpedo as the procedures are classified, but I can share one thing with you—the use of metal material fired out of the sub to confuse the torpedo. The torpedo would all of a sudden find itself pinging on multiple targets and not know for sure which one to go after. This doesn't always work, but it is always worth a shot.

After a lot of fancy maneuvering by our captain, the torpedo finally disappeared. Since we didn't hear it hit anything we had to assume that it finally ran out of fuel.

The crew was excited to know that we had avoided getting hit, but we were also wondering where it had originated. While deciding our next move, we received a radio message that informed us that we were accidentally shot at by one of our own submarines. We found out that a U.S. sub was doing practice drills with dummy torpedoes, and they went a little outside of their approved firing range.

Of course, our captain wasn't happy about the mistake, but he was glad that he didn't have a real threat in the area. One thing about those dummy torpedoes: except for not having any explosive material in them, everything else operates just like a real torpedo. So we had no way of knowing that it wasn't a legitimate threat.

The captained thanked everyone for a great job and then dismissed us so that we could go back to what we were doing. Of course, after the excitement, I knew sleep was not in the cards for me that night.

I have a couple of points to make in this chapter. The first one is that due to the massive amount of preparation that we went through with the numerous drills we conducted, the crew was ready for the challenge. Everyone did a fantastic job of executing their responsibilities. We were able to think clearly and not lose our cool during a highly stressful situation.

How prepared are you for life's difficult challenges? What if you lost your job for some reason? Are you prepared to go several months without an income while you find another position? What if you lost your spouse, and he or she was a significant bread winner in your house? Are you financially prepared to go on? What about retirement? Do you know how much money you will need to live the lifestyle that you desire? What if a fire broke out at your house? Does everyone know what to do?

Our submarine crew drilled constantly to ensure that we were ready for the challenges that came our way. Have you gone through any drills that address the critical areas I mentioned above? If not, I guarantee you that you will find it difficult to remain calm and cool, and this can negatively affect any critical decisions that you need to make quickly.

The other area that is key is communication. When the captain sounded the general quarters alarm, that meant everyone was supposed to report to their battle stations. They also call this an "all hands on deck" situation, although this is general Navy terminology because we couldn't exactly go top-side while under water.

The Navy knew that everyone would be in the right mindset when they heard the alarm. They would report to duty and then remain quiet while waiting further instructions from the captain.

Communication varied depending upon the situation. The officers were trained on when to use verbal or written communication in order to effectively communicate.

I believe that lack of effective communication is one of the major reasons that some companies fail. Email is used so much today that is seems face-to-face communication is becoming a lost art. The fact is, email isn't always the best way to get a message across. First of all, not everyone responds well to it. There are some people, often the more experienced employees, who prefer talking on the phone or in person. If you really want to be heard by them, you must change your communication vehicle to accommodate them. I have seen a number of times over the years where projects have failed because someone tried to manage it through written communication when not everyone in the group was wired that way. Have you ever had a situation where the ball was dropped because someone didn't pay attention to an email you sent?

The main problem with written communication is that there is so much more to the message than just words. Most studies show that the impact of words is only around 7% of the message. Meaning that the tone of our message and the non-verbal signals we send impact how someone interprets what we are saying more than just what we say.

Have you ever been in a situation where you misinterpreted an email? I know that I have received a few over the years that upset me only to find out that the person sending it didn't mean to come across that way.

If you manage other people you need to be keenly aware of the communication vehicles you use. I can guarantee you that if you like to hide behind emails and hardly ever spend time with your people, you will fail. Employees need to see their boss; they need to hear his or her voice. If you manage other employees then one of your core responsibilities is to motivate your team. There are many books on the subject of leadership, and many of them mention that a great leader can also be looked at as a great coach. Believe me, you can't coach from behind your computer.

The Navy knows how critical communication is to the protection of our country. They also know that effective communication is the sender's responsibility not the recipient's. When we fail to communicate properly it often leads to situations not unlike our torpedo in the water encounter. You spend your time trying to avoid all the problems that start coming your way. Sometimes we even try to trick these problems/torpedoes into thinking that the target is somewhere else. So avoid having to sound your personal *general quarters alarm* by communicating right the first time.

Summary

The greatest lessons to learn from this chapter are:

1) Your communication skills can make or break you.
2) Be careful of over-using email, in that words alone are not as effective at times when someone hearing the tone in your voice or any non-verbal messages that you are trying to send should also be included.
3) If you manage other people, they need to hear and see you. Try not to hide behind email.

4) If it is your message to convey, then it is ultimately your responsibility to get the message through. We sometimes blame others for not getting the message when we didn't do everything we could have to ensure it was delivered properly.

The Rudder

The rudder: a flat, vertically hinged piece of wood or metal located on the back (aft) of the submarine and on the outside of the hull. When traveling in water, the rudder is turned either right or left to steer the vessel.

"What's going on?" I asked my Chief.

The USS Stonewall Jackson had just taken a hard turn to the right when we were supposed to be traveling straight out to sea. This was my first time at sea on the submarine, and I was just learning the ins and outs of working in the navigation department.

"We have ourselves some visitors," the Chief explained, "and they decided to park right in our path."

The vessel in our path was actually a small Soviet surveillance boat. As I came to find out, this happened fairly frequently to U.S. submarines. It was 1982, and the Cold War was in full swing.

We often followed similar patterns out to sea until we found water that was deep enough for us to submerge. This gave Soviet boats a good opportunity to shoot as many pictures and video as possible before we were able to dive down and lose them. And every time we made a turn or tried to go around the Soviet boat, it would quickly maneuver to get back in our path. It was a game—but it wasn't much fun for us.

Our helmsman, the sailor in charge of turning the submarine and keeping it on course, had to make frequent right and left turns to avoid hitting this Soviet Navy vessel. The experience taught me that our boat's rudder was a crucial component for keeping us out of trouble and on the right course.

Since then, I've also learned that every one of us is equipped with a different sort of rudder that helps control our destinies. That's because it controls the words that we speak. That rudder is the human tongue. The tongue is only one small part of our bodies, just as the rudder is only one small part of the submarine. But like the rudder, it's an absolutely crucial component for keeping us out of trouble and on the right course.

I must admit that Chief Bruette didn't teach me this one. I have to credit the Bible, and more specifically, the book of James. James wrote about how little—yet powerful—the tongue can be, just like the rudder on a ship.

He also warned that our tongues can destroy our lives.

Do you agree that what you say can be a powerful thing? Do you agree that it can do a lot of good but that it can also do a lot of harm?

There have been many times that my own tongue has steered me straight into trouble. Sometimes it happens and I don't even realize it until later (usually Maggie will tell me), while other times I know just as soon as the words leave my lips. And undoing the damage of those unwise words is about as easy as turning a submarine around.

Recognizing the power of the human tongue is the first step to limiting its negative impact and maximizing its positive impact.

First of all, I firmly believe that the less we say, the less chance there is of making a mistake. There's an ongoing debate about whether women talk more than men. I'm no expert, but I'm pretty sure I know what anyone collecting data at my house would find. My wife Maggie and I often enjoy spending an evening with other married friends, talking over a leisurely dinner. Then the next day, Maggie will be on the phone with the same female friend she saw the night before and spend another hour talking with her about all kinds of different things! Believe me, I am not on the phone the next day talking to my buddy from the night before.

Those two hours we talked over dinner should cover us for at least a couple of months.

It stands to reason that the more you talk, the more chance there is of something being shared that could come back to haunt you. Gossip is a prime example of how destructive the little rudders in our mouths can be. It's often said that God gave us two ears and one mouth for a good reason, so we could listen twice as much as we talk. Very wise words!

Learning to listen more and talk less is good for our professional relationships, too. When we pay attention to what others are saying, we show respect. People like respect. Plus, people generally like to be around those who are attentive listeners. Next time you're at a meeting or party, make a point of asking people about themselves and getting their opinions on issues. People will love being around you. Everyone wins—you've made others feel good about themselves, and they think that you're a fun person, too. It's the perfect way to build rapport.

If we let it, our little rudder can be a tremendous help instead of a hindrance. Walt Wiley is the founder of a non-profit organization called Winning with Encouragement. He and his executive director, David Hodge, share a mission of turning people on to the idea of encouraging others. They stress that it's one of the best ways we can serve mankind.

I've worked for a wide variety of companies throughout my business career, including my own, SellEthics Marketing Group, Inc. If you spoke to my associates at any of those companies, I'm sure you'd hear a common theme—John is an encourager. This is a conscious choice that I made early in my professional career. No matter what environment I'm in, I choose to uplift others with my words.

My philosophy is simple. Think about what happens to a work environment when there is an encourager in the group. An encouraging tongue steers the group towards improved performance and greater productivity.

I received numerous promotions because management saw me as a "can do" person. Supporting others with my words has impacted my career in wonderful ways.

But that's not why I do it. For me, it's about talking to others the way I want to be talked to myself—with words of respect and support. I get great personal satisfaction from encouraging others and treating them with respect; I also believe I honor God by doing so. And the end result is that I have been well-liked throughout my business career as I climbed the corporate ladder in a way that makes me proud.

Trust me, if used this way, your tongue will never steer you wrong.

Summary

The life lessons to take from this chapter are:

1) The tongue acts like a ship's rudder; it can quickly change the direction of our interactions with others—for the better or for worse.
2) The more you talk, the more opportunities you have to say something that you might regret.
3) Try to listen twice as much as you talk. Show your interest by asking people questions about their lives and their work. Use your tongue like a rudder to steer the conversation back to the other person.
4) Find ways to encourage people around you. A simple "thank you" or a sincere compliment does so much to lift someone's spirits. And you'll feel good knowing you've encouraged a colleague or made a friend's day brighter.

Scheduled Maintenance

Scheduled maintenance: Every piece of equipment in the Navy has a planned maintenance schedule to ensure it is taken care of properly.

The term PMS has negative conations in civilian society as it does for any sailor ever born. But the meaning is different in the Navy: Planned Maintenance Schedule.

The Navy had a great recruiting campaign several years ago: *The Navy, it's not just a job, it's an adventure.* Now although I do agree that it was an adventure, there was one thing that my recruiter did not tell me—how serious the Navy is about everything looking good and running well.

This is where the planned maintenance schedule comes in. No matter what department a sailor would work in, there was equipment that would need to be maintained. When it was time to inspect a piece of equipment, we would have to grab the maintenance manual, go through the checklist (kind of like doing a car inspection), and then sign off that it was completed.

So although there was a lot of fun stuff to do and see in the Navy, a lot of time was spent keeping the inside and outside of the submarine in top-notch shape. Inspections were done frequently to make sure that the planned maintenance schedules were followed properly. If you failed to do so, it would make for a very bad day.

Why do you think the Navy is so serious about their maintenance procedures? Think about this for a minute before reading on. One of the first things that you might have considered is that they want to save money. This is true to some extent. But it isn't actually their own money—it is the taxpayers'. I'm not saying that they don't care; I'm just saying that it is only natural to not care as much about the financial aspect if it isn't coming out of your own pocket.

So what else then? One of the major reasons the Navy is so serious about proper maintenance is that most of the equipment in the military isn't for show. Meaning when they need it, they need it. It isn't just a nice-to-have but a must-have in order to protect the submarine.

Have you ever wondered how a submarine goes under the water? One moment we would be traveling on top of the water, and the next minute we were going underneath the water's surface. The way this happens is that there are large ballast tanks on board. These tanks are empty when traveling on the surface but when a submarine is ready to go under water, the chief of the watch opens up special valves that let water into the submarine but don't let the water out. The more water weight we would allow in the tanks, the deeper we could go.

Can you imagine what would happen if someone did not periodically inspect those special water valves that let water into our submarine? If one of those valves failed, the ballast tank would fill up completely possibly taking us to the bottom of the ocean. Of course, if the water were deep enough, we wouldn't survive because the pressure of the water would crush the boat. We would basically disappear with hardly any evidence that we were ever there.

So the primary reason for the PMS is that our equipment wasn't about luxury—it was about survival. Plus, we had to make sure that we could effectively launch nuclear missiles if called upon due to this being our primary purpose for existence.

There is another reason for having a planned maintenance schedule, and it is psychological. The captain knew that his crew would function better as a team if they took pride in their boat.

Pride overdone isn't a good thing, but I'm sure you can see how advantageous it is to have a crew that takes pride in their ship and individual departments—in how they look and how they run. It helps create a team spirit within the crew, and it helps motivate people to take pride in what they do.

The Navy's use of a planned maintenance schedule and the benefits behind it both intrinsically and extrinsically have direct correlation to the civilian world.

First, I have to ask you, what do you consider critical in your life that you make sure and take care of? Maybe you thought of your car and your house, or if you had your business hat on, you might have thought about your PDA or laptop computer. But have you thought about your most important asset? That's right—you!

There are a couple of simple reasons to take care of you. I'm sure you know these reasons but we tend to be better at knowing than doing. One reason is that there is only one of you. For the dads and moms who do everything for their children and sacrifice their own health in the process by running themselves down, I would like to remind you that the best thing you can do for your children is to be around for many years, because they will need you long after they have left the nest.

Ask yourself this question each morning when you get up: *What can't I afford to lose?* What if you lost your job? It happens to people every day. Sure it isn't pleasant, but you can survive it. There are many cases of people saying they are glad that it happened because it changed the course of their life for the better. What if for some reason your checking account was wiped out? No, it wouldn't be enjoyable, but in time you would have money back in the account. How about if you lost your home to a fire? It would be extremely disruptive, but in time you would have another home. Now the important question: What if you found out you had only six months to live?

Not a pleasant thought when we allow ourselves to go there, but I'm sure you get the point. There are many things that would not be fun to lose, but we could survive the loss. In many challenging situations, the people involved end up getting stronger than ever before, which helps them to live an even better life by making better choices for themselves from the lessons learned.

With all of this in mind, we need to remember each day that there is truly only one thing that we can't afford to lose and that is our life. I'm not saying that anything else isn't important, just that in the scheme of things we need to know where to prioritize our time.

So if you are in agreement with me that our bodies are truly critical to our wellbeing, then what should we do about it? If you created a planned maintenance schedule for yourself so that you looked and operated as well as possible and lasted as long as you could, what types of things would you have on your list?

I'm not going to spend a lot of time on the subject as there are plenty of great books on health and fitness. But to throw in my two cents worth, let me say that going on a diet is not a good idea.

People get on fad diets all the time. Why don't they work? It's because they aren't realistic. People get excited at first because they start losing weight, and then they realize they can't keep it up and gain the weight back (possibly more). To make it simple, eat the stuff you like but eat somewhere between 1,200 – 2,000 calories a day. Don't worry about any other measurement such as fat grams, fiber, etc. Always consult with your doctor first, but the reason we are getting more and more obese even with all of the light and reduced fat products on the market is that we consume more calories than we burn. It is that simple.

Believe me, if you follow the above calorie method you will lose weight. Your stomach will get back to its normal shape, and you will notice after a period of time that you aren't as hungry as you used to be. But looking good on the outside isn't enough. There are a lot of thin people in the world who are still not healthy, and that is because their insides are a mess.

We all need to exercise at least three or four times a week for at least thirty minutes. Once again, I'm not going to go into a lot of detail on this as other books would be more thorough in their explanations. But, our heart needs exercise. We must get our blood pumping through our veins in order to keep everything operating properly. No matter how thin we might look, if our cardiopulmonary system is not in good shape, we will not last.

The good news is that you don't have to go overboard with the whole exercise thing. Walking is great for you, so you don't have to worry about jogging. I personally love to run and have competed in various triathlons, but even I have to admit it has come at the expense of my ankles and neck. I have done a lot of pounding over the years, and it has taken its toll. I might have been better off just walking all of this time. But I have to admit I get such a high out of running that I am a bit addicted!

There are many ways to get your heart going, whether riding a bike in your neighborhood (especially up hills), playing catch with a football and running various patterns alternating who is at quarterback, going swimming, trying on some rollerblades. You will be much more inclined to stay at it if you find something to do that you enjoy and is realistic with your schedule.

I want to remind you why the Navy was so particular about their planned maintenance schedule: to enhance the effectiveness and longevity of their critical equipment and to create a sense of pride in the way the crew saw their submarine and their individual departments.

One common theme in this book is the value of self-esteem. I cannot emphasize this point enough: *You will become what you think.* There are always some exceptions to the norms, but in general, if you think good thoughts, good things happen. On the other hand, if you don't have confidence in yourself, you will end up with life's leftovers.

When we exercise diligently each week, we begin to take pride in ourselves. As I mentioned in my chapter about boot camp, there is something magical about having a sense of discipline. Discipline breeds good self-esteem, and good self-esteem breeds what? That's right—success!

So instead of feeling bad about PMS, make it one of your strategies for success.

Summary

The life lessons to take from this chapter are:

1) We must have a clear understanding as to what is truly critical in our lives and make sure we have a plan in place for taking care of these important assets.

2) The most important asset any of us has is our life. With this in mind, we must do everything in our power to prioritize taking care of it to the best of our ability.

3) Don't live to eat, but instead eat to live. I admit I love food. The problem is that most of us do not need more than 1,600 calories a day. If we do not burn as many calories as we consume, we will continue to gain weight.

4) Looking fit isn't enough. We must be in good shape on the inside as well. We must get our heart rate up three or four times a week for around thirty minutes. This keeps our very important heart muscle in good shape and our cardiopulmonary system working properly.

5) Don't spend so much time taking care of everybody else that you neglect what is most important—your health. Your employer, family, friends, etc., will all be

better off if you are around for the long haul.

6) Exercise must become a way of life. Once you have a weekly routine in place, you will start taking pride in the discipline you have. That will build good self-esteem, and you, in turn, will be successful.

Qualifications

Qualifications: Every job in the Navy and every promotion in rank comes with a list of qualifications which a sailor must meet in order to assume the assigned role.

As I mentioned in a previous chapter, when I was assigned to the USS Stonewall Jackson I was struggling with becoming submarine qualified. Fortunately, Chief Bruette helped me to overcome my mental block so that learning was never again a problem for me. The reason that this was so important is that a sailor's life is non-stop learning. Once you are qualified at one level, you are given a new list of qualifications to take you to the next level or pay grade.

The Navy was brilliant in its application of life-long learning. They clearly understood what each position required in skills and aptitudes, and they provided the training tools necessary for each sailor to achieve them. The Navy also realized the psychological value that life-long learning had on their sailors.

Think about it. Has there ever been a time in your career where you felt unchallenged? Going into work every day can be very difficult when you find your job to be boring. It is during these times that we become restless and start looking for opportunities with other companies. The Navy knows that they have to continuously challenge their sailors so that the job never becomes too boring. This is one of their major retention techniques.

Have you ever been in a job and wondered if and when an opportunity for advancement might come available? This can also be very difficult on your psyche, especially if you are the type of person who wants to move up the corporate ladder. Once again, the Navy understands this. They make sure that everyone has a realistic sense of how long they need to be in a particular position or at a particular level before they will be considered for advancement.

Have you ever been in a situation where you wanted to be promoted but no one had any concrete advice on how you could make it happen? In other words they couldn't tell you specifically what attributes or skills would be required for you to obtain advancement. The Navy doesn't want their sailors to be frustrated by situations like this, so they let everyone know exactly what it will take to make it to the next level (i.e., job knowledge, technological skills, training certification, etc.).

The business world could learn a great deal from the Navy's model when it comes to qualifications. In a study conducted years ago on some Fortune 50 companies, one of the common denominators of their reasons for success was their focus on employee training. These companies invested approximately 4.5% of their payroll budget into various training programs for their associates.

The reasons these companies felt a significant amount of investment in training was important is that it helped them: 1) limit their liabilities (i.e., diversity, ethics, etc.), 2) increase employee job satisfaction and morale, 3) reduce turnover, 4) adopt new technologies and methods, and 5) increase innovation. There are so many benefits to structured training curriculums that I find it difficult to understand why companies neglect it.

When we started SellEthics Marketing Group, we made a commitment to providing our associates with life-long learning. SellEthics University provides training not only in areas that will make them more effective at work (i.e., communication skills, computer skills, management skills, presentation skills, selling skills, etc.), but also in areas that will positively affect their personal life (i.e., health and fitness, home organizational techniques, personal finances, etc.).

Interestingly, some of our customers and clients have asked us to help train their associates. This isn't part of our business model as we are a sales and marketing agency, but it is something that we try to do when we can because of our commitment to the industry as a whole.

Continuous learning is truly a win-win situation for everyone—the employee as well as the employer. Even if your particular company doesn't have many training opportunities I hope that this book will inspire you to pursue self-educating. Just reading this book is a good indication that you care about increasing your knowledge and becoming a better you.

There are so many outstanding books to read, and if your community is anything like mine, there are also many opportunities to attend training courses through the town or through your local community college. In my area, Central Piedmont Community College has done an outstanding job of serving our business community not only in the content of their training curriculums but also the accessibility of the classes (i.e., nights, weekends, etc.).

The Navy realized how powerful their qualifications programs were to not only the morale of their sailors but also to the preparedness of the Navy in doing its job to protect our country. I have used many of the insights I learned from them in developing training curricula for our associates, and the results have been fantastic—exceptional skill levels, great morale, and low turnover.

Summary

The life lessons to take from this chapter are:

1) Companies that provide their associates with structured training curricula have a significant advantage over those who don't.
2) Training helps companies reduce turnover and risk while at the same time enhancing employee morale and innovation.
3) Offering employees training in areas of personal development (i.e., home organization, personal finance, relationship building, etc.) not only improves an employee's home life but it also makes for a better employee. When an employee is happy at home it affects their work life and vice versa.

Steady as She Goes

Steady as she goes: a nautical term used by the officer of the deck to direct the crew to maintain the present course and speed.

We were plotting our course up St. Mary's River in southern Georgia when Chief Bruette asked me about a particular section in the river. "How fast should we go through this winding section?"

"Well, the safest speed would be six knots," I replied. This translates into just faster than six miles per hour in a vehicle.

"That sounds pretty safe to me," he said. "We'll be turning every few hundred yards, so that speed should keep us moving at a nice steady pace to allow the sub to turn effectively."

Turning a large ship or submarine is no easy task. Unlike most vehicles, you need to start turning large sea-going vessels right or left well in advance of the turn. Just how long it takes for the submarine to turn depends on a variety of factors, such as how long the submarine is and how fast it's going, as well as the speed and direction of water currents. While learning to navigate a submarine, I wished that I'd paid better attention in my high school algebra and geometry classes. Those math formulas had a direct application when it came to turning a submarine successfully.

"Steady as she goes" is good advice for navigating safely and wisely, whether you're in a submarine or not. It's important to carefully assess the situation: should you pick up speed or maintain a nice steady pace? Often we proceed way too fast and run aground because of our impatience.

How many times have you jumped into a project, and then wished that you'd given it more thought beforehand? In order to be successful, we need to know when to slow down and when to crank it up a notch. It's never smart to go full speed ahead all of the time. It leads to poor choices and early burnout.

On the other hand, we also don't want to go too slowly. Have you ever missed a great opportunity because you were a little too cautious? Each of us has enormous potential. But it's difficult to reach our goals if we always proceed at a half-hearted pace, or worse yet, never cast off from the pier.

When the Chief asked me about my speed recommendation for St. Mary's River, there was a reason that I didn't recommend going slower than six knots. There had been previous instances where we slowed down to four knots in this part of the river to make sure we were safe. But we didn't this time. The tide was going out, and the speed of the current was close to three knots. Slowing the submarine down to four knots would have been a big mistake because our vessel would have lost all of its momentum. Turning the rudder at that point would make absolutely no difference; we would be dead in the water.

It's the same way with life. There is something magical about momentum. Imagine trying to move a one-ton boulder. Seems impossible, doesn't it? Well, if that boulder was already set into motion, it would have the forward momentum that allows you to keep it moving— steady as she goes. Put that same boulder on a hill (here's where speed can be dangerous) and then watch out!

I joined the Navy to escape my past. As you may remember, Bruette didn't think that was a great reason. But he did credit me for moving forward with my life. Like that rolling boulder, I was building momentum. Signing those enlistment papers set me in motion and changed my direction completely.

It's basic physics: if you aren't moving forward, you're moving backward. That's because with or without you, the world moves on.

Summary

The life lessons to take from this chapter are:

1) It's critical to assess each situation to determine the wisest pace for you to proceed.
2) If you go full speed ahead all the time, you will run aground or out of fuel.
3) If you proceed too slowly, you risk losing your momentum. You may end up dead in the water. Or you may actually move backward, carried by the tides and currents of life.
4) Steady momentum is the key to pushing forward and achieving your dreams. It allows you to make necessary course corrections safely.

The Crew

The crew: Depending on the size of the vessel and its mission, a crew is assigned to help run the ship and participate in battle stations when engaged in a fight. My particular submarine had around one hundred and forty sailors on board.

If I could go back and change anything from my military experience, I would have been more tolerant of my fellow sailors. I was young and I had my own naive perception of what to expect out of other people, so I missed out on some good relationships back then.

Of course, I did have a few buddies who I am in touch with from time to time. One of them, Danny, owns a restaurant in the mountains of Tennessee called The Farmer's Daughter. It is only open Thursdays thru Sundays, and the food is fantastic. From their barbequed ribs to their marinated pork chops, it is some of the best food I have ever tasted. And that explains why I have seen Danny more than any other of my other Navy buddies.

I didn't realize back then that people have different personalities that make them a better fit for certain responsibilities. We had all kinds of different jobs on the submarine. To prepare a submarine to go out to sea and keep it operating while out, it takes administrative personnel, cooks, people to drive the sub, people to navigate the sub, people who know how to shoot a torpedo, people to fix leaks, people to keep the engines running, people to keep our nuclear power plant operating and safe, people who could fire off nuclear missiles, people to keep our radio equipment running properly so that we could receive and interpret encrypted messages, people to listen to ocean sounds to ensure no one was sneaking up on us, people to keep our computers operating properly, people to keep our mechanical mechanisms running properly, people to order enough food and supplies so that we could hide under water for a few months, etc. These different jobs required people with different personalities and skill sets to keep things running properly.

It sounds so simple, but I just didn't get it back then. I still struggle with it a bit today. The problem is that people like people who are most like them. If someone is an aggressive salesperson with an outgoing personality, then he or she typically will enjoy hanging out with other people who have a Type A personality.

Someone who might be more reserved and who works in accounting probably would not typically enjoy going out to lunch with someone from sales.

I spoke with a friend of mine who is struggling at work. He is the smart, analytical type, and his boss is an aggressive salesperson. He performs very well at his job but when promotions are being handed out, he is often passed up. You want to guess what type of person his boss likes to promote? That's right, aggressive people. If he worked for someone who was quieter and more analytical, he would have a better chance of being promoted.

We shouldn't get angry about the fact that people generally stereotype and like to associate with people who look and think the same way they do. It has been going on for thousands of years. The important thing is that we learn to respect this reality and to work within it, because it isn't going away.

One of my business partners and the president/CEO of our group, Joel, has a different personality than mine. We have a similar belief system and most of our business philosophy is right in line, but he is a hard-charging Type A personality who is a born leader. He loves to be in charge. He has an opinion about everything, and of course he usually thinks his opinion is correct. I have to admit, it usually is.

I'm a bit different. I don't enjoy conflict as much as he does. I am okay with taking a back seat at times and letting others take charge. I am basically a little more laid back than he is. We are both extremely competitive, but I typically hide my competitive spirit while he wears it on his sleeve. What you see with Joel is what you get—he is wide open. I'm more difficult to read.

Joel and I have worked together so long that we have come to respect our differences and laugh about them (on occasion!). We have also realized that together we are a fantastic combination. My personality and skill sets help compensate where he is lacking and vice versa.

The problem with everyone's personality is that our greatest strength is also our greatest weakness. Joel's aggressiveness in business, which has helped the company grow substantially year over year, is also what turns some people off. Due to different personalities in the workplace (both internally as well as externally), not everyone is going to like Joel. But the fact is, he is an amazing leader. Employees of ours who might not always understand his aggressiveness admire his strong work ethic and discipline towards everything in life. I believe that if you live a life of integrity like Joel does, it makes it easier for people to look beyond your personality shortcomings, because the good so much outweighs the bad.

My strengths are in my analytical abilities, creativity, and people skills, but I have to tell you that I am not a great salesman. I'm good behind the scenes putting presentations together, but I don't enjoy going out and making sales calls. I think the main reason that I don't enjoy the sales side is that I am a bit of a control freak. I like to have my agenda (to-do list) and work it. The problem with sales is that you can start your day thinking you are going to get various things done and then one phone call from a buyer and your day is shot. You're running around addressing what he or she wants you to get done.

You also have to have a pretty thick skin if you are in sales. The fact that a prospect turns you down means he or she doesn't think that your product or service is the best fit for their needs; at least, that is what you should think. I would be more inclined with my personality type to take it personally and think they were rejecting me. After a while I would logic my way through it. The fact is our personalities are what they are, and this can lead to certain tendencies of which we should be aware.

The different jobs on our submarine required people with certain tendencies as well. That is why the Navy does so much personality profiling to determine who might be a good fit for the submarine service. As you can imagine, they certainly do not want someone who is claustrophobic. Once the hatch is closed and the submarine submerges, we stay under for typically weeks at a time, sometimes much longer. You definitely don't want to have anyone on board who gets a sudden urge to feel the wind on his skin.

Sonar men on the submarine were an interesting breed. They would typically sit in a small space, almost like a large closet, put a headset on, and listen to ocean sounds for six hours straight. They had computers as well that they would watch to see if any sounds were picked up that they didn't catch on their headsets. Sometimes they would hear animal sounds like shrimp or whales, while other times they would hear a legitimate contact such as one of our own ships or a Soviet submarine. These sonar men were so talented, they could sometimes profile the sound of another vessel and know exactly what it was—sometimes even whose boat or ship it was. They could do this because certain vessels have certain sounds (called signatures) that they put out because of how they were built. As you can imagine, sonar men were crucial to the safety of our submarine because they kept us moving away from any other vessels that might be trying to find us.

My question to you is: What kind of a person would you want sitting in a quiet room for six hours straight, not talking to anyone but instead listening intensely for any contacts that might threaten the sub? The Navy figured out that they would be better off having the quiet, analytical type doing that kind of work versus people with outgoing personalities who loved to interact with people. As I mentioned at the start of this chapter, I wish I were wise enough back then to know this. I just figured people who worked in that department were weird.

It takes all kinds of people to make an organization operate smoothly. I have learned to respect the various differences in personalities and skill sets instead of getting frustrated by them. I have also learned how important it is to get the right people in the right positions, because it only leads to frustration all the way around when you don't.

Summary

The life lessons to take from this chapter are:

1) People have different personalities and most people like to be around others who have a personality similar to theirs. When we do this, it limits our world. We need to learn to enjoy everyone around

us. Life is much more enjoyable and our opportunities become more abundant when we learn to respect and focus our attention on the good attributes in everyone and not focus on the bad traits also in everyone—including ourselves.

2) We must be cognizant that whatever personality our immediate manager has, in most cases he or she will look to promote people who are similar. I'm not saying it can't be overcome; it is just a reality with which we must learn to deal.

3) No personality is perfect as there are pros and cons with each. It is important to recognize this, because we sometimes think that we would be perfect for anything and this isn't true.

4) Realizing the above point, we must recognize that our particular personality might be better suited for certain things. If you aren't the type of person who is okay with dealing with conflict and don't particularly like networking/ socializing, then you probably wouldn't enjoy a job in sales. Whereas if you have an outgoing personality and just love networking with other people, then you probably wouldn't be good at sitting at your desk for eight hours analyzing data.

5) It isn't good for you or your employer to be in a job where your personality and skills aren't a good fit. The money is never worth the stress that you endure trying to survive in the wrong environment for you.

6) It takes a crew to run a ship. We would not have successfully fulfilled our mission if there were a bunch of John Mann's running around. If you want to be a great leader, you must realize this and not fill your organization with people just like you.

The Mission

The mission: Our mission on board the USS Stonewall Jackson SSBN was to stay undetected by both hostiles (the enemy) and friendlies (U.S. ships and allies) so that if the President of the United States authorized a nuclear strike, we could proceed undeterred to the depth necessary to launch our nuclear missiles.

Ping! Ping! I couldn't believe what I was hearing. It sounded just like it did in the movies. Another vessel had detected us. The captain quickly called back to the sonar room to find out what was going on. Apparently our sonar equipment was a little slow in activating after a turn that we had taken, and it didn't catch the contact before it found us. At this point we didn't have a clue who it was. It could have been one of our own ships or possibly a Soviet submarine. But either way, our mission was always clear—stay undetected.

The captain told the helmsmen and planesmen (the two crew members who steered the submarine and made it go up and down in the water) to begin evasive maneuvers. This entailed not kicking up too much of a stir in the water by avoiding drastic speed changes and instead trying to slowly go even deeper into the ocean and find a thermal layer of water in which to hide. These thermal layers are sudden temperature changes in the water, creating a layer that impedes sound travel thus hampering the effectiveness of sonar devices. Captains often used these thermal layers (also called Thermoclines) to avoid detection, and we were in need of one desperately. The captain also told the crew to rig for silence, which means no one was to do anything (including talking) that might create a sound.

We proceeded to go deeper into the water while still hearing that haunting *ping* sound. After sinking several hundred feet, we stopped and listened. The control room was eerily silent. After several minutes we didn't hear another sound. We were safe this time around.

Records are always kept on everyone's vessel, which also includes all of the contacts that we came across at sea. Once we got back to port the captain had to attend a debriefing. It is never good news if the captain finds out that another U.S. ship identified us during their mission at sea. The captain, knowing his primary mission was to travel undetected, did not want a blemish on his service record, so this meeting was always an important one. Of course on the flip side, he was able to report all of the contacts that we snuck up on at sea, and believe me there were many.

It was so important for all of us to know our primary mission, as it dictated all of the strategies and tactics we would deploy in preparation for and while on the mission. We were known as the *silent service*. Our ability to run *silent* and *deep* was so critical that every time out we went out to sea, we would first test how well everything was stored on the submarine. This was typically done soon after we were in deep enough water to go up and down in the ocean. This particular drill was called *angles* and *dangles*. The angles we would take were very steep, so I would usually hold onto to a pole in our control room to prevent myself from sliding into someone else's department. It was an absolute nightmare for the cooks who always had a tough time keeping their pots and pans stowed tightly enough that when the submarine went into a deep dive, they didn't crash all around the kitchen. I can't tell you how many times I heard loud cursing coming from the mess hall when we practiced those drills. We wouldn't stop the *angles* and *dangles* drill until everything was completely silent when we did them.

As I entered the business world, I took what I learned from the Jackson on the importance of knowing your mission and applied these ideas everywhere I went. It was critical, as it helped me develop strategies and tactics in my various roles that would help the company achieve its stated mission/objectives. Now, as an owner of a company, I make sure that everyone in our organization clearly understands what our mission is and how each and every one of them can both positively and negatively impact what we are trying to accomplish.

Our stated mission for SellEthics Marketing Group is, "*To deliver results with ethical solutions.*" This means a couple of things. First of all, it means that at the end of the day we are all accountable for positive results. It doesn't matter how much someone might like you, in the end you have a product to deliver and/or a service to perform. If you can't do it, they will find somebody who can.

Our mission statement also lets everyone know that the end does not justify the means. If one of our associates has to deceive someone to get the business, then it isn't worth it. Our associates know that they cannot lie to anyone—internally or externally. The truth might hurt sometimes because there is no way we can be perfect all of the time, but it is more important to us than the business itself. We feel that if we can't do business in our industry the *right* way then we need to find another business. We refuse to compromise our integrity. We know that at the end of the day, our reputation is all we have.

In fact, I came up with the name SellEthics for a reason. It helps all of us remember what we have to live up to every day. Believe me when you call yourself SellEthics you better live up to it, or your competition would have a field day shooting torpedoes right into you.

Living up to our name isn't always an easy thing to do. I admit there have been times when I've been tempted to compromise. It's tough when you come to the realization that your particular business model might not be right for a particular client. The money is out there and you start thinking, *Well, it may not be perfect but maybe we can fake our way through it.* I'm not saying that it is rational, but it is human nature. I always end up coming to my senses, though.

You see the fact of the matter is, no amount of money is worth destroying your reputation in the marketplace. The end result if I had comprised would have been a client who was not happy with our services and then would have left, telling everybody about the bad experience. Plus, I would have to live with myself. The thing about compromising your integrity is that it will not go unnoticed. Once your employees see you selling out in order to get the business, then they, too, will think that it is okay to do whatever it takes to win. Talk about becoming a terrible role model. I want to make sure that each and every night I can lay my head down knowing that I have nothing to regret.

Our company also has a goal and it is, *"To be the best in the eyes of the people we serve."* We serve a lot of people. We serve our clients—that is a given—but we also serve our own employees. Each year we send a confidential employee survey that gives everyone an opportunity to rate the company in various areas. One of the things we ask is whether SellEthics is the best company for which they have ever worked. Our scores are actually outstanding, but we will never be happy until every single one of our associates can honestly say that we are the best.

We do a lot of things to try and make it a great place to work. I typically call all of our associates on their birthday and company anniversary. There are even a few of them that I call on their wedding anniversaries to remind them to get some flowers for their spouse. We send all of our associates hand-signed birthday cards from the management team. I am constantly sending out thank-you notes along with gift cards for jobs well done. We send everyone a check at Thanksgiving to help pay for their family meal. Probably one of the best things we do for them is that we share our profits with everyone in the company. The owners made a vow when we started the company never to take money out just for ourselves. The fact is, we all work hard, so we all should benefit when we have a good year. Fortunately, we have been blessed every year we have been in business, so everyone has enjoyed a profit-sharing check a couple of weeks before Christmas.

I hope you see from the above that when we come up with a goal, it isn't something just to have on paper. We take it very seriously. We want to be the best. Nothing else is good enough. Even if every single one of our associates and clients said we were the best, we won't let up. There is only one way to stay on top and that is to stay hungry—never be satisfied.

I'll wrap up with our company's purpose: *"To glorify God by operating the company based upon Christian Biblical principles."* The owners of this company are all Christians, but we come from different denominations. We all agree that there is no perfect denomination, just a perfect God in heaven. When we started the company we wanted to do it with integrity. We felt there was a tremendous need in our industry for ethical behavior. We made the decision to be honest with everyone with whom we dealt, that we would treat our suppliers (i.e., equipment, office supplies, etc.) and our associates with a great deal of humility and respect, and that we wouldn't let the pursuit of money cloud our judgment.

There are other companies trying to do the same things we are, so we don't think that you can only be an ethical company if you are Christian-based. We just want everyone in our company to clearly understand the *reason* behind why management has determined to conduct business in an ethical fashion.

I hate to admit it, but the owners aren't perfect. We have made and will continue to make mistakes. We just hope that our associates realize that we *want* to be perfect. We want them to be proud of us. Their opinion of us matters.

Realizing that we aren't perfect is a critical component to our company's success. This is due to the fact that we don't try to make it on our own without our employees' input. We know we can't be successful without them. We don't have all the answers, and we know we need to tap into their experiences so that we can make better decisions for our company. We know that the moment our associates are afraid to tell us how they honestly feel about the direction our company is going, we will begin to fail.

We have to be willing to accept employee feedback—even if it's criticism. I have to admit that when someone rises to the top of a company, a bit of ego is often in tow. I am not immune to this human deficiency. With this in mind, it isn't pleasant for me to hear that my idea isn't good or that someone likes my idea but has a better solution. I hate to admit it, but it is true. I would love to think that my way is *always* the best way, but it isn't. It gets a little easier to swallow over time (although it still gets caught in my throat a little), but the more you learn to accept criticism the stronger you become.

Summary

The life lessons to take from this chapter are:

1) Every organization should have clearly defined goals, mission, and purpose.
2) Everyone in the organization should clearly understand how their particular role in the company affects these areas. If associates cannot clearly communicate how they can either positively or negatively affect the company's goals, mission, and purpose, then either they weren't communicated well, they are too complicated, or the associate just doesn't care enough to know.
3) Never take on an attitude of "good enough." Don't accept anything but the best from yourself and your team

members. The moment you sit back on your laurels you will become a target of your competition.

4) Never think you have all of the answers. Never lose touch with the people in the field. My favorite skipper (Captain Wolverton) always made sure he made the rounds and that he was approachable. He knew how important it was to understand the reality of his situation. He listened to the experiences of his crew, and that is why he became an amazing captain.

5) Don't let your ego get in the way of becoming the best you can be. I know it is hard to admit that your ways aren't always the best ways. But believe me when I tell you that your personal and professional growth will be stunted as long as you hold on to the fantasy that no one knows you have any weaknesses.

The Harbor Pilot

The harbor pilot: One who is called upon to take control of a large vessel and navigate it safely when it is traveling to and from a port where navigation is extremely difficult due to the number of hazards or adverse weather conditions. A harbor pilot has expert knowledge of a particular section of water.

Even though I was our submarine's primary navigator and I was called upon to navigate the submarine any time we were traveling in dangerous waters, my expertise wasn't always enough to ensure the submarine was safe. There were times when both the officer on deck and I had to turn control of the submarine over to a harbor pilot. This can be a bit of an ego hit in that we were basically saying that someone could do it better than us, but it was worth it. I always had a sense of relief when we turned over controls because I had a tremendous amount of confidence in these individuals.

This same principle applies to life as well. We can't be the best at everything all the time. There are times and areas of our lives that would be better managed by someone else who has greater expertise. There are many examples of this.

One area that most people should get assistance with is personal finances. Few people do a good job of managing their money. Financial counselors/planners spend their time educating themselves on a variety of strategies and tools for people in various circumstances. I don't know about you, but I don't find financial planning interesting. With this in mind, I don't typically waste my time going to seminars because of my lack of interest. I might as well tap into the expertise of someone who does enjoy this area and has become an expert in it.

These financial advisors are like harbor pilots in that they have honed their expertise in a particular area and they can help you safely navigate through what is sometimes a complicated topic.

Another area where someone else's expertise might be beneficial is in how to create a great marriage. Let's face it, from early on we attend school and learn about all kinds of different subjects, but we don't typically attend any training on how to have a great marriage. Most people just try to wing it. This is probably why we have such a high divorce rate in this country.

Someone who is trained in this area can provide tremendous insight into not only what a marriage is supposed to be but also what it is not supposed to be. Men and women are different. It is critical to understand these differences and how to work with them instead of trying to change them—which isn't going to happen. Our behaviors can be tweaked, but our overall makeup isn't going to change. Marriage counselors can help couples appreciate the good and how to deal with the bad that is part of everyone's marriage.

Just like my stress was reduced knowing I had a harbor pilot to turn to, all of us have experts we can turn to as well. I feel like some of us are afraid to admit that we don't know everything and need help. We shouldn't be embarrassed—our education, experiences, and personalities make us better geared towards handling certain things than others.

I'll share with you one quick but embarrassing story of when I should have called in an expert and didn't. I hope you can learn from it. First, let me start by letting you know that I am not the greatest handyman. My brother can do anything when it comes to building or fixing something. When he got all of those genes from my father, there were apparently none left for me. But, it doesn't stop me from trying.

My wife knows that I am not the greatest when it comes to fixing things, but every once in a while she will give me a shot. She does regret doing it one evening. Our kitchen faucet had a leak, and Maggie was going to call a plumber. We were sitting around the living room discussing the topic, and I talked her into letting me give it a try. When she said yes, I was in such a state of excitement and shock that I went running to get my toolbox. Now, my little red toolbox isn't the size that I would want to break out in front of any of my male friends. But, it typically works for the limited jobs that I get myself into. In my excitement over getting to fix the sink, I forgot the number one thing you must do before working on a faucet. Any guesses? That's right, *turn off the water supply!*

What happened next was like an episode of *I Love Lucy*. I started working on the faucet, and the next thing you know I had what looked like Old Faithful going off in my kitchen. Water was shooting straight up into the air as high as the top of the kitchen cabinets. Of course, Maggie was in the living room with no idea at this point what was going on in the kitchen. I did what any college-educated man would do at this point: I put my hand over the gusher thinking this would somehow magically stop it from spewing. This only sprayed the water over me and everything in the kitchen. By then it was too late to cover things up. Maggie heard the commotion and made her way to the kitchen. I'll never forget the look on her face when she walked in and saw my hand over the gusher and water spraying all over the place.

Of course, she had to ask me the inevitable question: "Didn't you turn off the water supply?!" How humiliating! By then water was all over the floor, and it was slippery linoleum. (She now has hardwoods in there—I wonder how she negotiated that deal.)

Anyhow, I was in such a state of panic that I blanked out on where the water cutoff was to the house. I went running around like a chicken with its head cut off while at the same time dialing a good friend of mine (Chuck) who remodels homes. He of course came flying over to my house with a real toolbox to literally bail me out of the situation.

After all was said and done, the parts to the faucet had flown all over the place and the faucet was unrecoverable. I then had to call a plumber to not only fix the mess that I had created but also to install a whole new faucet. Several hundreds of dollars later, we had the kitchen back in shape. Needless to say, Maggie has not authorized my involvement in any plumbing projects since then.

There is a clear moral to this story and that is—let the experts do it. I thought I was saving a few dollars doing it myself and ended up paying dearly—although it has given

Maggie a great story to share with friends and neighbors over the years. At this point, I think she would say that the money spent was worth the entertainment value it is now providing her with at my expense.

Summary

The greatest lessons to learn from this chapter are:

1) You cannot be the best at everything so don't waste your time trying.
2) Know when to turn critical components of your life over to those who are harbor pilots in a particular area.
3) We cannot experience happiness or success in our lives unless we learn to let go of personal ego and get a grip on what we are good at and what we are not. First, it is too stressful to try and do everything yourself. Second, we can be much more successful by learning to tap into the expertise of others. This keeps us from running aground and keeps us moving successfully forward on life's journey.

The Ocean

The ocean: Approximately 71% of the earth's surface is covered by water. Most of the water can be found in both the Atlantic and Pacific oceans. More than half of the ocean is 9,800 feet deep (1.9 miles). The tallest mountain on the planet is not Mt. Everest (which is 29,028 feet high) but instead Mauna Kea, Hawaii, which is 31,000 feet high. Only a third of it sticks out of the water.

"You have got to be kidding me, we are going out in this?" I said to Chief Bruette.

"The captain [not Captain Wolverton] thinks we can make it, and he wants to get to the practice range so that we can work on torpedo firing drills," replied the Chief.

We were in Cocoa Beach, Florida, at the time, and the weather was terrible. It was the day after Thanksgiving, and the waves were humongous.

Much to my dismay, we took off out of port, but we didn't get far. The waves became so big that they started crashing over the top of the submarine and knocking us to the bottom of the ocean. The problem was that we had three sailors on top of the submarine (the officer of the deck and two lookouts). They were tied in with harnesses to keep them from washing overboard. Each time a wave would crash down on us, a big stream of water would come pouring down the hatch into the control room where I worked. We eventually had to batten down the hatch and leave the men up there.

The captain turned the vessel so that we could better absorb the impact of the waves, and then we opened the hatch to see if the guys were still alive. I was surprised that they were. They were able to untie themselves and crawl down the hatch. They were soaked, and they looked beaten up. Some of the equipment was damaged. Our large mast headlight (it's like a really large light pole) on top of the submarine had snapped in two.

The waves hitting the submarine knocked us all around the control room. So much water had made its way on board the sub that electrical equipment began shorting out. We were in big trouble. We finally limped our way back to port and had to stay there for a few days in order to get all of the equipment fixed. I believe our captain got into a little trouble over that one.

The ocean is a powerful thing. It doesn't matter how well prepared you are, you can't control it, and it can change at a moment's notice. The song by Gordon Lightfoot, *The*

Wreck of the Edmund Fitzgerald, did a great job of describing the horror of dealing with an uncontrollable storm. I'll never forget that one part of the song: "At seven p.m., a main hatchway caved in. He said, 'Fellows, it's been good to know ya.'" Haunting lyrics!

While navigating the submarine, we had to pay close attention to what the ocean was doing. It didn't matter which direction we pointed the sub and how fast we were going, inevitably we would end up off course because the water beneath us was always moving. There were some areas like the Gulf Stream, which runs up from the Gulf of Mexico and travels off of the east coast all the way up to Newfoundland, that had a speed of around four knots. If someone were fishing along the Gulf Stream and they turned their engine off, in just a couple of hours they could end up close to eight miles further north than where they were supposed to be. As I mentioned earlier, this event of being moved by ocean currents is called *set and drift.*

The whole concept of set and drift relates to life as well. No matter what direction you think your life is headed, you will be taken off course. We don't live in a vacuum. No matter what we do, there are uncontrollables in play.

Nationwide Insurance has a great commercial series where the theme is: "Life comes at you fast!" It is so true. Stuff happens. None of us is immune to the possibilities of getting laid off, losing a loved one, not having the nest egg that we hoped, etc. These things have been going on for ages. Nothing will happen to you that hasn't happened to someone before. So no matter how hard you try to make plans for your future, life will have an affect on it.

The ocean is a great metaphor for life in that no matter what you do, you can't control the environment around you. The only real thing you have control over is yourself and how you will handle different situations. The problem is that we get frustrated trying to control things that we have no control over.

Think about how frustrated we can get at times by our boss, our children, our co-workers, our family members (in-laws and out-laws), our friends, the traffic, the weather, etc. Although we can't control these people or things, we let ourselves get frustrated by them. Take traffic for example. Have you ever been in a big hurry and it seems like every driver on the road is out to get you? And haven't you also noticed during these times that the traffic lights all seem to turn red? Next thing you know you are pounding on the steering wheel and yelling at other drivers. Some people actually stick their hand out the window and tell other drivers that they think they are "number one"—if you know what I mean. It isn't worth it. There is no need to get frustrated over it as there is nothing you can do about it. Or is there? What is the one thing that we could have done differently during those times when we are running late and experiencing all of those traffic problems? That's right, we could have left earlier.

The ocean, like life, can change at the blink of an eye. One moment you think everything is going along pretty well, the next someone in your family develops cancer. I visited one of our associates who has been on long-term disability for several months due to cancer. He is a great employee and everything was going just fine. All of a sudden, he started getting real tired. One day he told his wife that he couldn't go to work as he barely made it out of bed. The two of them went to the emergency room, and they diagnosed him with cancer. Of course, his entire life changed. He had always been a hard worker, and now all of a sudden he has been cooped up in his home and in hospitals receiving chemotherapy. Believe me, his priorities have changed from the experience.

This kind of thing happens all the time. There isn't anything we can do about it but deal with it when it occurs. The ocean, like life, can be calm one moment and then horrendous the next. No one has a life free from trouble and strife. The formula for life is $E + C = R$ (Events + Choices we make = the Results). Stuff will happen to us. The important thing is how we respond when it does.

This doesn't mean we need to be afraid of life. It is a journey where there will always be good days and bad. Have you ever thought about why life is cyclic? The reason it is cyclic is that we would not appreciate the good times if we didn't have bad times to use as a reference. The fact is, we don't typically grow personally, professionally, or spiritually when things are going great for us. It is during those times of struggle that we tend to develop our character. So we need to embrace life, both the good and the bad, realizing that in the end we will become better and stronger.

Summary

The life lessons to take from this chapter are:

1) The ocean, like life, is uncontrollable.
2) No matter how hard we try, we will be taken off course when it comes to the direction our life is headed.
3) We must learn to control the controllables and let the rest of it go. We can control ourselves, but we cannot control other people or most of the events of life that come our way. By making good choices, we can limit the bad experiences, but no matter what we do, we will always have good days and bad.

4) We don't grow personally, professionally, or spiritually during times of comfort and convenience. It is during times of difficulties that we experience the most growth.

5) Life is cyclic for a reason. We need to learn to embrace it fully and appreciate the good days when they occur and realize that bad times will pass. Sometimes we allow ourselves to get into such a rut that we forget that the bad times will cycle through and that better days are ahead. The problem is that people make major life decisions during the down cycle, and it typically leads to poor choices.

Batten Down the Hatches

Batten down the hatches: When seas get rough, the officer of the deck uses this command to order the crew to secure anything on deck that isn't tied down and also to close any hatches that might let water into the ship.

All sailors know this term well, because stormy seas are inevitable. Rough seas can pop up at a moment's notice. There is so much water to evaporate that the sky becomes humid and drops the rain molecules back into the ocean. Even when we knew a storm was coming, it was sometimes so large that we couldn't outrun it or go around it. So we had to ride out the storm.

Many things are hard to describe, and riding out a storm is one of them. Imagine this: You're looking straight in front of you and can see way out into the ocean. All of a sudden, you feel the hull beneath your feet drop. The next thing you know, you are staring at a wall of water a couple of stories tall. Then, just as suddenly, you start rising back up, the wall of water disappears, and you can once again see out into the distance. The constant up and down while rolling from side to side causes many sailors to get down on their knees and re-embrace their faith.

Any time I would experience rough weather at sea, I would hang on to the mindset that *this too shall pass*. In other words, I knew I just had to hang in there, because eventually the storm would pass and the sea would be calm again.

Life is a lot like this. One moment things are going along all nice and calm, and the next all heck breaks out. Have you been there? Sometimes we can see the storm brewing a little ways off in the distance, while other times it just sneaks up on us. Either way, it is a rough ride.

Have you faced any storms this last year? My family had our share. The biggest one for me was Maggie going through her tenth spine surgery. She has some deformities in her spinal column, and it has had to be reconstructed several times and tweaked here and there for various reasons. This time she had to wear a brace, which has kept her from driving for a couple of months. As of this writing, she still had one month to go before she could get behind the wheel.

Needless to say, it has been a trying time for us both. She has struggled with a lot of pain and being cooped up in the house, while I have been running around gaining a much greater appreciation for all she does to keep the household going.

Even though we have been challenged by several things over this last year, it doesn't come close to what other people have faced. One of our associates (Scott Elam) lost his sixteen-year-old son Brandon after a three-year battle with cancer. Brandon was one of the most amazing young boys I have ever met. His smile would light up a room, and he always showed genuine love and compassion toward everyone he met.

I can't even imagine what Scott and his wife Anita are going through. They just had their first Christmas without Brandon, and now they will have to deal with his birthday along with both Mother's and Father's Day. They have established a memoriam of Brandon which you can find at: www.brandonelam.com. It is a beautiful story.

It is a tragic situation, but this kind of thing happens all the time. They feel blessed that they got to say goodbye to Brandon, and they feel so sorry for parents who don't get that chance due to various tragedies that occur.

That is life, and none of us is immune to it. We will encounter storms of various degrees. Some are small, while others can feel like riding out a hurricane. That is where battening down the hatches comes in. On any seagoing vessels, there are points that are vulnerable to water. These points are hatches, which allow sailors to pass from the outside of the hull to the inside of the vessel. In a storm, sailors are given the command to protect the boat by closing these hatches and locking them down.

So how do we protect our vulnerable points during those times when we face rough seas? One point of vulnerability that we have during difficult times is our reaction to the event. Too often people make rash decisions during stormy times, and that is the worse thing they can do. You can batten down this hatch by being careful how you respond to a problem.

First intuition for some people is a good thing, but the problem is that when times are rough, our emotions negatively affect this unique ability. Fear and anger often set in, both of which cause our decision making to lose some of its effectiveness. The best thing to do is patiently think through the matter and not jump into anything to soon. Patience is absolutely key in effectively riding out a storm.

Another area of vulnerability is when we think we need to handle the issue ourselves. We are not alone. There isn't anything that you and I will go through that someone else hasn't already experienced. I know that Anita and Scott turned to someone else in our community who had recently lost her son to cancer. She was instrumental in helping them understand all of the things that they would be going through. I remember on the morning that I saw Brandon for the last time (he died that evening), this sweet woman was by Brandon's side helping to clean him up when he threw up blood. I can't imagine how much comfort it brought the family to have someone right by their side with her sleeves rolled up, helping to comfort in any way that she could.

We need to remember when we are going through stormy times that we can effectively protect ourselves through seeking advice from others. For me, I always have God, whom I can turn to in times of need. The peace I get in knowing that no matter what comes my way, God will see me through, is a crucial component in the overall happiness that I have in my life.

We need to keep in mind that we can batten down this critical hatch by inviting others in during our time of need. We shouldn't feel guilty about it either. People want to help. I consider it a blessing when I get the chance to help someone in need. I think I get more out of it than the person I'm helping.

Another way to protect ourselves during the storms of life is remembering that we shouldn't run from our problems. There are a couple of reasons why our captain never tried to run from a storm. First of all, the submarine could more effectively handle the massive waves when we confronted them head on. This is due to the fact that the front of the hull is more aerodynamic, meaning there is less surface area to hit. The worse thing he could have done was turn the vessel broadside where there was more area to be hit by a wave.

Another reason that he didn't run is that it was pretty much useless. Storms move fast, and it would eventually catch up with us anyway. The best thing to do is to get it over with. If the captain didn't, and the storm caught up with us, we would get pounded while he tried to turn the vessel around to where we were facing it head on.

Storms of life are inevitable. The best thing we can do is batten the hatches and keep in mind that this, too, shall pass.

Summary

The greatest lessons to learn from this chapter are:

1) Everyone experiences problems in life.
2) We need to face our problems and not run from them.
3) We need to make sure we don't make any rash decisions during difficult times. First intuitions aren't always the best answer due to this ability being negatively affected by anger and fear.
4) We need to remember that we are not alone. There are always people we can turn to for help and, even more

importantly, there is a God whom we can always turn to in our times of need.

5) There is calm before a storm, and there is calm after one as well. We need to keep in mind that no matter what bad thing it is that we are going through, things will get better.

The Gyrocompass

Gyrocompass: A navigational instrument used on boats and ships that provides the direction of true north (the direction of the earth's rotational axis) versus magnetic north (often used with regular compasses) so that the crew knows in which direction the vessel is traveling. Magnetic compasses aren't as effective in that the environment around it can negatively affect its readings (i.e., certain metals, copper wire, etc.).

Once our crew went out to sea, we would periodically receive encrypted radio messages from the on-shore command to proceed to various destinations. They would typically send us places where no other vessels were, but every once in a while we would receive a message to meet up with other Navy vessels in order to perform military exercises.

"Can you imagine trying to meet up with the other ships through using the stars to navigate?" asked Chief Bruette. "Back in those days, they would be lucky to get within a couple of miles of each other. Then they would travel back and forth trying to spot one another. Thanks to innovations like navigational satellites and the gyrocompass, our jobs are much easier today."

He was right. By the time I made it into the world of navigation, technology was a major factor. The navigational satellites would give us our latitude and longitude so that we knew exactly where we were, and then the gyrocompass would tell us exactly where we were headed.

The Chief added: "The Chinese actually invented the use of a magnetic compass way back in the 1300s. They used the compass to let them know where magnetic north was so that they could use it as a reference point when traveling at sea and help them find their way back to port. The magnetic compasses they used weren't as good as our gyrocompass, but it gave them a decent idea as to what direction to go."

I always found it interesting that when Chief Bruette spoke about the gyrocompass that he had complete faith in it. He often used the term *true north* when he described its accuracy. With how massive the ocean was and with no landmarks to reference while in the middle of it, the gyrocompass was crucial in getting us from one point to the next as there wasn't a lot of margin for error. For example if we pointed our submarine at a heading of 090 degrees (which is directly east), and we traveled a few hundred miles only to find out that the compass was incorrect and we were actually headed 095 degrees, we would end up thirty miles or so off course.

Can you imagine what kind of chaos there would be at sea if vessels didn't have an accurate directional heading? Trying to coordinate military operations would be impossible without our gyrocompass providing a true north indicator.

You might be asking yourself at this point, what does this whole gyrocompass thing have to do with real life? Good question! In order for the gyrocompass to be effective, everyone had to agree to its widespread usage. In other words, if we navigated our vessel using true north as 0 degrees and the British fleet thought it would be best to use some other point of reference, how could we ever find one another at sea if we were coordinating joint operations? It would be virtually impossible. We all had to agree upon one standard—one truth that everything else would be based upon. Is it sounding more like real life now?

In order to prevent chaos on earth, God created one *truth*. This truth is inside each and every one of us from the moment we are born. You may or may not agree with me on this, but I believe that as infants we were already programmed to know that some behaviors are wrong. I believe we know from birth that we shouldn't hurt someone else. I believe that we know we shouldn't take something that does not belong to us. I believe that we know we shouldn't say "no" to our parents. I believe that we know we shouldn't lie. What do you think? Do you think these are learned insights, or do you agree with me that we seem already programmed to know certain things?

Each of us seems to have this internal gyrocompass (moral compass) that points us to the direction of certain truths. It is when we deviate from our internal gyrocompass that our lives become chaotic. If you think about it, God built this internal mechanism so that we would know that it is more important to sacrifice self-interest for the betterment of society as a whole. In other words, he wanted us to know that it is more important to serve others than it is to run around looking for opportunities to be served by others.

God wants us to know right from wrong inherently so that we can make good choices for our life. Think about how great our lives would be if we used our moral compass more often. The fact is, most of life's troubles come from when we do things for selfish reasons (i.e., buy expensive things to show off, cheat to get ahead, lie to get out of trouble, etc.).

I believe that God knew he couldn't count on mankind teaching moral principals.

Civilizations/societies come and go, so he made sure that each of us was given the same opportunity via our own internal gyrocompass to know what is good and what is bad. He also made sure we had a reference book (The Bible) with the Ten Commandments in the Hebrew Testament, the beatitudes in the Gospel of Matthew, and the golden rule of them all: *to treat others like you want to be treated*, in order to reinforce these moral truths.

It is pretty amazing to think that throughout the history of mankind, there were and are today certain truths that govern societies. Why are there laws against taking something that doesn't belong to you? Why is there a law that we can't kill someone? Why can't we beat someone up that we don't like? From the moment we were created, we had this little something inside letting us know what is *right* and what is *wrong*. Can you imagine how chaotic life would be if God didn't design it this way?

Summary

The life lessons to take from this chapter are:

1) None of us has any excuses for not making good sound moral decisions because each of us was given an internal

compass that points us towards the truth.

2) It is when we deviate from using our moral compass that our lives become chaotic.

3) God knew our lives would be more fulfilling if we understood it is better to serve than be served.

4) A moral code has existed from the beginning of mankind. It is this code that allowed societies to grow successfully.

5) Research has shown that most civilizations that disappeared did so due to a lack of moral conduct. This negative conduct included: 1) The leaders began taking advantage of their citizens to the point where the citizens had to overthrow the government; 2) The civilization began growing to a point where they would attempt to conquer another society for what they had (i.e., food, land, slaves, etc.); 3) The civilization was conquered by another society greedy for what they had. Very rarely were societies completely decimated by natural causes. Failure to follow God's moral code was typically the reason for the decline of various civilizations.

The Patrol

The patrol: This term is used to describe when a submarine is no longer in its home port but instead fulfilling its duty at sea.

It was early in 1985 when I left to complete my final patrol. I could only get one more in due to the fact that I was scheduled for an honorable discharge in May. I had considered staying in the military because there were so many advantages to it (i.e., my comfort and familiarity, job stability, pay, etc.), but I could not help but think that I would always regret it if I didn't go to college. I knew that once I finished college, I could always pursue getting my commission as an officer in the Navy through officer candidate school, so I had a back-up plan.

A couple of days before I went out to sea I stopped by Maggie's apartment to drop off some of my personal stuff. She asked me where I would be staying since my apartment lease was up. I told her that I was planning on sleeping in my car for a few days and going by the base in the morning to shower and shave.

I actually lived in a car for about two weeks earlier in my Navy career with a buddy of mine (Barry Blanton). We wanted to save money and the timing of our lease and when we were taking off to sea, just didn't match up well. I think we lived off of Bojangle's biscuits and chicken the whole time. The funny thing is that we kept getting moved all night long as various police officers would knock on the window and ask us what we were doing. So the sleep wasn't good but we were saving a lot of money! During this time we also hung out a lot at a fitness club where we were members so that we could watch TV, use their showers—oh, and work out from time to time.

Of course, when Maggie found out that I was going to live in my car for a couple of days she would have none of it. Next thing I know, I'm sleeping on her couch (I really was) and being fed great meals. Her cooking was so good that I ended up marrying her later that year. We have been together ever since. During our many years together I have also made it back to my humble beginnings a few times—the couch!

It is hard for me to describe my last time out at sea. I wanted to cherish everything about it. For those of you who have been in the middle of the ocean, you know how indescribably beautiful it is. Nothing was more peaceful to me than when we would travel on the water's surface in the middle of the night. If I wasn't on duty, that was where you would find me—that is, if I could talk the officer of the deck into letting me hang out with him and the lookouts. Usually they were accommodating. My favorite parts were the sound of the water gently rolling over the bow of the submarine and the stars that were so thick it didn't even look like there was any space between them.

I had tears in my eyes my last time on top of the sail (although I hid them well) because I knew that it was the last time I would experience that kind of beauty and peace. I remember reflecting on the fact that I probably wasted a lot of time in the military due to my particular mindset. You see, any time we would go on patrol, I would quickly get focused on the destination. Since we had nuclear warheads on board, our opportunities to pull into various ports were limited, but we still had a little fun. If we weren't stopping in a few of our U.S. ports like Kings Bay, Georgia, or Ft. Lauderdale, Florida, we were sometimes directed to places like Halifax, Nova Scotia, or the island of Barbados. Once I knew where we were going, my focus went to the destination. I would count the days, hours, and minutes, to when we would arrive, and of course I would daydream about the fun that I would have on shore.

What I realized while reflecting on my time in the military was that I became so focused on each destination that I forgot to enjoy the journey. I would typically have a great time in port, but it was always short lived and then we were out to sea again. The fact is, we were mostly poking holes in the ocean hiding from everyone, so most of our time was spent engaged in the journey not at our point of destination.

This whole concept of forgetting to enjoy the journey finally sunk it when I got into the business world. From the moment I got my degree I was a fast-tracker. I would go to work somewhere and figure out exactly what promotion I was going for, and I would make it happen. I set benchmarks where I wanted to be salary-wise, and I would achieve them. I can still remember the first time I went over $30,000 a year. I was so excited. I'll also never forget the first time I was promoted into management and got the big corner office and my own secretary. I was ecstatic! But guess what, the excitement was extremely short lived. I found myself looking around, thinking, *What's next?* It was the same feeling I had in the Navy when we made it to port somewhere. The fun would last for a little while, and then I was ready to move on and see something else.

It's not just me. I have spoken to hundreds of extremely high achievers in my lifetime, and the story I hear is often the same. *Is this all there is? Certainly there is something better out there somewhere! What's next?* Does this sound familiar to you? The problem with having this mindset is when will it end? When will you finally be satisfied? Will it be when you finally have a salary over $100K or when you can say you made your first million? Will it be when you can finally move into that country-club neighborhood you have been admiring for years? I don't mean to burst your bubble, but those things will not satisfy you for the long term.

Everyone should have destinations/goals in their mind because that is what inspires us to get up every day and make things happen. But we can't lose sight of the fact that this life of ours is a blip on the radar screen. I told you earlier about my friend Brandon Elam, who I lost to cancer. I saw him the morning on the day he died, although I didn't know it was the end of his journey. I just felt the need to see him. He was clear that he was ready to go. He was ready to go to heaven and finally get rid of the pain.

He said that he had a great life—no regrets. Sure, there were some things that he would have liked to have done but it was no biggie, he had a lot of fun while on earth and he knew he was loved by so many people. The only thing he was worried about was how his mom, dad, and sister would deal with losing him. He wanted them to move on and have a great life.

To remember him, but not grieve for him. Just focus on all of the fun and the love that they all shared. What an awesome young man!

Brandon provided a great example of how to enjoy the journey. He had personal goals in mind that he wasn't able to achieve, but to him, that was okay. The fun was in the pursuit. He liked to make other people feel good. He was very unselfish. His goal was always to make the best of each day.

Until we wrap our minds around this concept, we will always be restless. Nothing, and I mean nothing, will ever be enough. As I think back to my time in the Navy and the number of wasted days looking ahead to the next port versus getting the most out of the entire experience, it makes me sad. Chief Bruette knew how to enjoy the journey. He made the best of each day and didn't go looking too far ahead for his next fix of joy. I just couldn't grasp the concept back then.

I'm glad that it has finally sunk in. It is a strange feeling when you finally come to peace with who you are. I'm no longer worried about what is next on the horizon. I'm still goal oriented, but it isn't my entire focus any more. As a matter of fact, I created my own personal mission for each day. Every morning while traveling to work I ask God to help me with my personal mission. This is how it goes: *"God help me to be a great role model for people around me personally, professionally, and spiritually. Help me to be faithful and true to both you and Maggie in my thoughts, words, and actions. Help me to by unselfish, patient, loving, kind, compassionate, humble, wise, joyful, and hopeful.*

My goals/destinations in life are still in full swing, but believe me when I say; I won't be completely disappointed if they don't work out. If I can accomplish my own personal mission each day then I'll be happy. It helps me to enjoy this short patrol of ours called *life*.

Summary

The life lessons to take from this chapter are:

1) Our destinations/goals are crucial in helping us stay motivated, especially in a business environment.
2) In most cases when we achieve a goal (i.e., new car, new job, etc.), the initial excitement eventually goes away and then we start looking for something else to pursue.
3) To enjoy life to its fullest, we must learn to enjoy each day. If our mind is always focused ahead then there will never be that feeling of satisfaction from realizing that there is something to be gained right where we are at that moment.

4) I guess a good way to look at it is like when we play sports, football for example. If someone scored every time they got the ball, eventually it would become boring even if it was your own team. The thrill is in being in the game and going through the ups and downs and then every once in a while scoring that touchdown. Scoring is an important part of the game, but there is also a lot of excitement between the goal posts. We need to learn to enjoy those first downs when we get them. We need to realize that our competitors will score on us from time to time. We need to understand that sometimes we should get a new game plan together because the one we are using isn't working out. Life is a game, with each day filled with both good and bad. Our goal should be to keep plugging away and enjoy the scores when we get them. But more importantly, enjoy the game itself and the competitors and teammates who make us stronger.

All Ahead Full

All ahead full: the order given when the captain is ready to open up the throttles and let the vessel run as fast as she can. The captain will only do this when the boat is in open waters and there are no water hazards to worry about.

The beauty of having your engines cranked up is that there is a sense of freedom. It's hard to describe, but even if you aren't going anywhere in particular, it's fun to get there fast. Maybe it is a guy thing.

Plus, when our engines were at "all ahead full" it caused much larger waves rolling across our bow, and this is very inviting to dolphins. Dolphins love to catch air. By heading straight towards the submarine, they would catch a wave off of our bow, fly way up into the air, and then make a big splash when landing in the water. Then they would speed up and get in front of the sub to do it all over again.

Lastly, the water in our wake was beautiful when the screws from the submarine kicked it up. The middle of the Atlantic Ocean is dark blue and gorgeous. For some reason it gets even more beautiful when the screw from the submarine churns through it and adds air to it. It seems to add some green to it but the end result is fantastic.

I hope after reading this book that you have a decent understanding as to both my character and personality, because they are the key reasons why I wrote this book in the first place.

My life has been blessed beyond anything that I could have imagined and certainly beyond anything that I deserve. One of my personal missions is to help others experience the happiness and success that I have been able to achieve.

I think that God wired me to hurt when I see people holding themselves back. I've met so many people over the years that I know are capable of great things but just like me at one time, they don't see it. Some of them grew up in tough circumstances and never made it to college, while a lot of them had so many negative people in their lives that they finally gave in to believing that happiness and success are for a select few.

Rulers throughout the ages have used this mentality to hold people down. They knew that if they could somehow create an image that their family was born with something special inside that made it their birthright to succeed, that the commoners would accept their place in society.

What do you think? Don't you see the similarities in the so-called "ruling class"? Does someone have a leg up if they are born into a wealthy family? In some ways yes, but in other ways no. Yes, they often have a better chance of making it to college. Yes, their family often has a business network, which opens doors. But then why is it that some of the most successful people in business (i.e. Bill Gates, W.K. Kellogg, Estee Lauder, etc.) came from modest backgrounds?

There are no excuses, no legitimate reasons why someone does not have the ability to accomplish great things in his or her life. There might be some people who have lost their chance; but for most of us, it isn't too late.

This book was written so that people can learn to let go of all of the junk that has been tying them down and give them direction for how to navigate their way to a great life. It's not for everyone. Not everyone has the desire to go out and experience the world. As I mentioned earlier in the book, that is okay as long as they are content being tied to the pier watching other people come and go. But how sad it is, when someone is capable of such wonderful things and they never come close to reaching their potential.

At the end of this life, I guarantee you that all of us will have some regrets. There is a common theme among most senior citizens who share their life experiences. One of the biggest regrets you will ever hear from any of them is that they wish they would have risked more. One might tell you that she wanted to open up her own bed and breakfast, while another might say that he wishes he would have pursued an idea for an invention he once had. Some might say that they should have pursued a management position but were afraid to take on the challenge. It's sad to hear their regrets.

We must learn from them, or we will find ourselves years from now in the same boat. Few people will ever tell you that they tried something that they wish they hadn't. Usually these people who have tried and failed learned something from the lesson that helped them later in life. There is a sense of satisfaction knowing that they took on the challenge.

Life is too short. There is so much to see and experience, if we will only take the chance. I admit that it is a bit scary to untie the lines and start pulling away from the pier. It is scarier still to head out to sea and lose sight of land. You begin to feel a vulnerability that is hard to describe. But I promise you that it is worth it. The confidence, freedom, and excitement you'll feel as you venture out into the unknown are indescribable.

One thing that you will begin to notice is that there aren't many people out on the seas of life. The adventures are boundless but the adventurers are few. You'll find that most people are still back in port waiting to hear the stories from those who were brave enough to go outside of their comfort zone.

I'm so glad that I had someone like Chief Bruette in my life to help me let go of the lines that were holding me back. I'm so glad that my favorite shipmate (Maggie) is still journeying with me after all these years. I've already accomplished so many dreams that I'm running out of new goals. I still have a couple that I know I must accomplish so that I don't end up with any of the "I wish I would have's" so I still have more adventures ahead.

I hope I see you out there on the high seas. I'll be the one with a big smile on my face, gazing at the beautiful stars, counting my many blessings with a big wake behind me as my engines are kicked in at all ahead full.

One last nautical term for you: *Godspeed!* (Defined: May you have a successful journey!)

Scuttlebutt

Scuttlebutt: The water cooler on ships where sailors often gather to share information or gossip. Scuttlebutt therefore has become a term for gossip or rumors.

This chapter was written to provide a little more insight into what life was like on a submarine. If you have a weak stomach, you might want to pass on reading the paragraphs about disposing of our waste. Although it has a very funny story tied to it!

Work environments have a lot in common with one another, whether you work in a high-rise office with great views of the city or in a 425-foot-long submerged submarine with no outside view at all. There will always be good days and bad—so I recommend mixing in as much fun as possible, without getting into trouble.

Here's the scuttlebutt:

Life on the USS Stonewall Jackson was surprisingly good. For one thing, our cooking staff was one of the best in the Navy. I think that was because the military realized that life on a submarine can be difficult enough without having sailors upset about lousy food. Except for fresh dairy and produce, which only lasted a few days at sea, our food was excellent quality—although we did eat way more chipped beef than I liked.

When it was time to load food onto the submarine, it was an all-hands event, meaning that everyone on board had to pitch in. Our supply officer checked off the supplies as they left the supply ship, and the boxes were then passed down a long line of sailors, from the top of the submarine all the way down to our mess hall. I was always stationed in the navigation department, near the bottom of the hatch. This proved to be a great location. Every once in a while a box of cashews or peanuts would end up slightly lighter by the time it reached the kitchen.

Snacks aren't typically available toward the end of the tour. When we'd open our stash a couple of months into the patrol, we were heroes among the crew standing watch with us. But if any Navy JAG officers are reading this, let me make one thing very clear—I'm not exactly sure how the cashews got into our department. It has been years now, and my memory is a little foggy.

For me, one of the best parts of being at sea was that mundane chores that we had to do while in port (like laundry and bill-paying) were taken care of for us. Of course, this came at a cost—the ultimate one being the lack of female company.

Women weren't assigned to submarine duty because of the incredibly close quarters. Space was cramped, due in part to the massive amount of equipment needed to keep the submarine running properly. Passageways were so narrow that we had to turn to the side to let someone by.

Our sleeping quarters were similar to those you'd find on a train. I slept on a small bed with a thin mattress, called a rack. These racks were usually stacked three high, like three coffins sitting on top of one another. Each had a curtain, giving crew members a little bit of privacy. Sleeping hours usually ran from 7:00 P.M. to 6:00 A.M., and the sleeping quarters were kept dark at those hours to help people rest.

These living conditions taught us respect for one another's limited space. It's no wonder that the Navy does so much psychological profiling—they don't want people who can't get along with others on board a crowded submarine.

To get an accurate impression of what it's like to live on a submarine, imagine that you've moved into an impossibly small apartment, and for three months you can't leave the place or even look out of the windows. Remember, there are no windows on a submarine. When we were heading toward the surface, the best I could do was look out the periscope—and all I ever saw was a bunch of blue water.

Now, imagine walking around in your undersized, over-packed apartment as it moves up and down, and rolls from side to side. Getting used to this sensation is referred to as "getting your sea legs." It takes some practice, but eventually I learned to walk a pretty straight line with the floor rolling beneath me.

How long the Jackson stayed submerged was based on the particular operation. Sometimes we surfaced a couple of times during our three month patrol, but there was an especially long patrol when we were involved in some sticky dialogue with the Russians. If I remember correctly, we stayed submerged for seventy-seven days straight. To not be able to see the moon or sun or feel the wind on my face for that period of time was very tough.

My work schedule was supposed to be six hours on shift and twelve hours off. But it didn't always work out that way. For instance, if I had the midnight watch, I worked from midnight until six in the morning, giving me only two hours to eat and get ready for my 8:00–5:00 day shift. I didn't have a chance to sleep until six o'clock that evening, making for an eighteen-hour day. (As it turns out, this was great training for the work hours I'm putting in these days.)

Even if the work load wasn't heavy during my shift, I had to remain available for all-day practice drills, department meetings and training sessions. And if I wasn't navigating, there was still plenty to do, thanks to the captain—who loved to see his submarine shine.

But there was also time for relaxation on the Jackson. Individual headsets allowed us to listen to all kinds of preprogrammed music. Twelve different stations, from country music to rock, offered us choices. Of course, after a while I would begin to hear the same music playing over and over again.

We also watched movies on board the submarine. The crew's mess (dining room) was the biggest area, so that's where we pulled down a large screen to run the projected movies. These movies weren't the most current hits, but we liked them just the same. Our favorite (during these early 1980s missions) was *Honeysuckle Rose,* with Willie Nelson. We watched it so many times we knew the script and the songs by heart. Sometimes we got carried away with our enthusiasm—that is, until an officer stuck his head into the room. He didn't have to say a word—believe me, his "look" told us all we needed to know.

People have asked me how we were able to breathe while the submarine was submerged. While it's true that the air on board turned to carbon dioxide as we exhaled, we were actually able to manufacture our own fresh air. Special equipment, called CO2 scrubbers, took the bad stuff and turned it into very clean oxygen. This manufactured air was so pure that the first time the submarine surfaced and I opened the hatch to breathe in the "fresh" outside air, I was revolted. It smelled disgusting! It always took about twenty minutes to get used to regular air again. Some of the air-purifying technology we used at that time is now being used in home air-cleaning devices.

We also created our own drinking water with special distillers that took ocean water and made it safe to drink. Unfortunately, this was a slow process, and sometimes our water supply became very low. During these times, we went into a rationing mode, which meant no showers. An unwashed sailor is not someone with whom you want to share cramped quarters.

Which brings us to a couple of other dirty topics. First, people wonder how we got rid of our trash. The answer, while not environmentally friendly, is simple—we shot it out of the submarine. Food and garbage were compressed by a giant compactor and smashed into metal tubes, a couple of feet in length. At an appropriate depth, we'd use 700 pounds of air to shoot the garbage out of the sub. The trash would immediately begin sinking to the bottom of the ocean, where the immense water pressure helped it disintegrate.

Next is the even nastier subject of our sewer. Submarine toilets look much like those in our homes, except that they're made of metal and are much more heavy-duty. Just as it does on a bus or an airplane, submarine waste from the flushed toilets goes into a sanitary tank. At the same time that we disposed of our garbage, we also used the 700-pound air to flush out our sanitary tanks.

In order to not disrupt life on board any more than necessary, we usually flushed these tanks in the middle of the night. During this process, we posted signs so that the crew would know not to use the rest rooms. But inevitably some poor sailor would join what was affectionately known as the "Stonewall Jackson's 700 Club."

It was easy to join. It began with waking up in the middle of the night and missing the signs. After using the toilet, a sailor would reach down to flush, pulling a special valve that looked like the lever on a slot machine—a maneuver that positioned his face right over the toilet. Not only did the unsuspecting sailor end up wearing what he had just deposited, he was also covered with everything else from the sanitary tank.

Our system was a closed one, designed for the water to be blown out through the sanitary tank and out the hull of the sub. When the sailor opened up the valve, it gave the sewer another place to shoot. I can't begin to describe how funny it was. First I would hear a loud noise followed by a scream. I have to admit, I never could resist running to the restroom to see how bad the sailor looked. There he'd be, standing soaking wet in the middle of the rest room, covered with all kinds of nasty stuff and cussing up a storm. It was absolutely hilarious!

To add insult to injury, the new 700 Club sailor couldn't shower until we were finished blowing the sanitation tanks. For him, waiting for the showers to open up probably felt like an eternity. News spreads fast on a submarine. During this time, more and more crew members, having heard about his misfortune, would stop by to make sure he was okay (if you know what I mean).

Living, working, and yes, playing on the submarine taught me to look for the good along with the bad. I learned that there are always ways to ease a stressful or difficult situation. On the Jackson, we did it with camaraderie and healthy doses of humor. We respected one another's space and personal tastes in music. But we gathered together on a regular basis to share movies and laughs and, of course, some good-natured scuttlebutt at the water cooler.

Take care and may *peace* be with you!